The

# Ozark Trail
# Guidebook

Hiking, Mountain Biking, Horseback Riding

**Margo Carroll & Peggy Welch**

First Edition

Published by Enjoy the Journey, LLC
First edition, first printing
Library of Congress Control Number: 2005900134

Book designed and all Photos by Margo Carroll and Peggy Welch
Cover photo: Along the Courtois Creek Section
Printed in the United States of America
Enjoy the Journey, LLC
PO Box 358
Pacific, MO 63069
www.ozarktrailguide.com

ISBN 0-9761231-0-X

# Dedication

If…

…some time spent in the forest rejuvenates you…

…you have ever gone for a walk in the woods and stopped to admire an old tree, placed your hand upon it's bark, and marveled at it's strength…

…your parents instilled in you a deep love of nature, and you share that with those you know…

…you pick up trash as you go, and leave none of your own behind…

…you have done at least some small part to preserve our natural resources…

…you have ever helped to build or maintain a trail so more people will get out there to appreciate the wild areas, and commit to preserving them…


…then this book is dedicated to YOU!

Bluff top view of the Eleven Point River on the
Eleven Point River Section of the Ozark Trail,

# Acknowledgments

The Ozark Trail is an outstanding natural resource that thousands of individuals have made possible. We would like to thank those who had the initial vision, and all of those who have worked on the trail since the beginning. There will always be more work to do on the trail, so we would also like to thank those who will continue to support, build, maintain, and love this trail. A special thanks to the members of the Ozark Trail Council for their guidance and support of this project.

Thank you to Patti, Deb, John, and the many other hiking friends who joined us for some of our trail "research"! We enjoyed your company and inspiration. Cooki, we're so glad you got to share some of our adventure. Thank you for the laughs, the love, and the support. And thanks to Peggy's Dad, for encouraging her love of the outdoors. When she got tired out there on the Ozark Trail, she just kept telling herself that the end was "just around the bend". . . .

Trail marker and blackberry bushes along the Current
River Section.

# Contents

Crossing the Courtois Creek on the Courtois Creek
Section of the OT.

# *Introduction*

You are holding the first ever guidebook for the Ozark Trail! The information for this guidebook was gathered as the authors hiked and mountain biked the Ozark Trail. Detailed information was collected by using GPS mapping units, taking digital photographs, by making digital voice notes and sound recordings.

Conditions on the Ozark Trail change on a daily basis. New roads are built, roads are closed, logging operations take place, and areas along the trail get overgrown. This book is simply a tool to help with your journey on the Ozark Trail. Remember that conditions change. This is not meant to be your only resource for navigation. A set of USGS Quadrangle maps (topos), a GPS unit or compass and the skills to use them are strongly recommended.

The Ozark Trail is a backcountry multi-use trail that today spans over 340 miles through beautiful Missouri countryside. When completed, the OT will extend from St. Louis to the Arkansas border where it will someday connect with the Ozark Highlands Trail.

This guidebook has detailed information and maps for each of the fully constructed sections and some information for incomplete sections of the trail. Trail section information is organized in a north to south direction, except for two sections. The Taum Sauk Section is probably the most traveled section of the OT and most hikers (not open to mountain bikers or equestrians) travel this as separate day hikes. The information is organized into three sections that reflect the most popular traveling directions. The Victory Section is organized east to west.

Even though the Ozark Trail is a work in progress, there are many miles that are finished and await exploration. The Missouri landscape that the OT traverses is hardly considered a mountainous landscape. Most of the 'big' climbs along the way are only a few hundred feet. There are just a few climbs that are higher than that.

Mountain biking on a warm spring day.

-The Ozark Trail Guidebook

# How to Use this Guide

Each section chapter begins with the mileage and symbols that represent the permitted trail users for that section. Some sections have restrictions on only part of that section; these are noted in the section heading.

**About this Section-** A brief description of the section and highlights along the trail

**How to Get There- Trailhead Parking Areas-** Directions to each of the trailheads located on that section. An overview map is included to assist as a reference.

**Trail Description-**Describes the trail section, and gives detailed notes, GPS and mileage. Landmarks, locations for trailside camping and possible water sources are noted.

**Maps-** Lists the USGS Quadrangle maps for the section. Note: There is an overview map at the beginning of each section. A more detailed section map is included with the trail description.

**Camping Facilities-** State and Federal campgrounds near the Ozark Trail. Many of these campgrounds only provide primitive facilities. Detailed information on facilities and seasonal operating dates can be accessed at the campground website. A list of websites is provided at the back of this guidebook.

**Nearest Towns and Services-** The Ozark Trail does not pass through any towns. Services can be few and far between. The towns nearest the trail with services have been listed.

**Contacts-** Lists the land managers for that section. The Ozark Trail travels through lands managed by many agencies and landowners.

**Possible Day Hikes-** Suggestions for shorter hikes.

# Ozark Trail Council
## Trail Use Guidelines

Camp at least 100 feet from the trail, water, and scenic areas. Leave your campsite so no one will know you were there.

Treat all water used for drinking or cooking.

Use a backpacking stove for cooking and build a fire only if absolutely necessary. Do not build fires on edges of bluffs, on glades, or in caves. If a fire is necessary, clear the area of combustible material. Use only small material that can be broken by hand to burn, make sure you drown the fire before leaving, and scatter or bury the ashes. Do not encircle the fire with rocks.

Do not camp in glade areas.
Glades are extremely fragile ecosystems.
Intrusions can be devastating to these beautiful areas.

Bury all human waste at least 100 feet from the trail, streams, or water impoundments. Pack out everything else you packed in.

Use caution when crossing streams. At times during high water and floods, stream crossings are impossible to negotiate.

Enjoy plants in their natural setting. Do not collect plants.

Be considerate of others: respect the rights of private landowners and remember that solitude is also a resource to be protected.

# Trail Users

## Hiking
All sections are open to foot travel.

## Horseback Riding, Equestrians
Over 239 miles of the Ozark Trail are open for equestrian use. The Taum Sauk, Current River, and Blair Creek Sections do not allow equestrians, and the first 9 miles of the Courtois Section that travels through the Huzzah Conservation Area are closed to equestrian use. The remaining 239 miles offer the horseback rider great opportunities for day rides and longer rides. Trailhead parking areas that provide enough area to accommodate vehicles with trailers are noted in the section chapters. Some sections of the Ozark Trail are very popular with equestrians, including the Wappapello Lake Section, the Victory Section, and southern part of the Courtois Section that includes the Berryman trail. The Mingo Saddle Club maintains much of the Wappapello Section.

## Mountain Biking
Sections that are open to equestrians also allow mountain biking, and over 239 miles of the Ozark Trail are open for mountain biking use. The Taum Sauk, Current River, and Blair Creek Sections do not allow mountain bikes, and the first 9 miles of the Courtois Section that travels through the Huzzah Conservation Area are also closed to mountain bikes. The remaining 239 miles offer the mountain biker great opportunities for day rides and longer rides. The southern part of the Courtois Section is the most popular with mountain bikers. Gateway Off Road Cyclists (GORC) has adopted part of the Ozark Trail.

## Thru-Hiking, Mountain Biking, Horseback Riding
Soon, when the Middle Fork Section is completed, the Ozark Trail will offer those looking for an extended "thru" trip the opportunity to travel over 210 miles on the trail. Currently the Ozark Trail does not have trailside shelters or other amenities that the Appalachian Trail or the Ozark Highlands Trail offer. The remote route of the OT will add to the difficulty in resupplying on a longer trip. But where there is a will, there is a way, and we look forward to the upcoming years and the initial "thru" trips that will establish the protocol for long distance trips on the Ozark Trail.

## Shuttle Services
Shuttle services come and go. At the time of publishing only one shuttle was serving portions of the Ozark Trail. For updated information on shuttle services please check www.ozarktrailguide.com

Ozark
Trail

# History of the Ozark Trail

The Ozark Trail began as a vision in 1977 by Federal and State land management agencies.  Construction on the trail began shortly after and today over 340 miles of the eventual 500+ miles of the trail are completed.  The original design for this long distance trail has the trail beginning south of St. Louis, near Arnold, traveling along the Meramec River in a southwestern direction to the Ozarks, where a scenic loop has been added, and then continuing to the Arkansas border.  The dream is to link the Ozark Trail to the Ozark Highlands Trail in Arkansas, making a long distance trail of over 700 miles.

Work is currently being done in the St. Louis area along the Meramec River corridor and on the Middle Fork Section that is located in the Mark Twain National Forest near Bixby, Missouri. The new Middle Fork Section is being constructed by the U.S. Forest Service and volunteer crews.  This section is scheduled to be finished in late 2005.  When the Middle Fork Section is completed the Ozark Trail will feature a 210-mile 'thru' section.

# Safety on the Trail

The Ozark Trail offers a chance to explore many wild areas. Within any wild area, there are potential hazards. Be prepared against possible hazards:

## Planning a Hike

Plan ahead. Good planning makes for a more enjoyable trip. Check the weather and get all the updated trail information possible. A USGS topo map is indispensable while traveling the OT. These maps are available at: Mark Twain National Forest, 401 Fairgrounds Road, Rolla, MO 65401, 573-364-4621 or from the Missouri Department of Natural Resources, Division of Geology and Land Survey, P.O. Box 250, Rolla, MO 65401, 573-368-2125. The Ozark Trail travels through some of the most remote areas in the Midwest. A GPS unit or a compass is a must. Learn how to use these navigation tools, and if using a GPS unit, take extra batteries.

## Trail Markers

The Ozark Trail is marked with a green and white OT trail marker. Also, silver diamond markers may be encountered along the trail. These diamond markers are being replaced with the green and white OT markers for more consistency along the trail.

## Hunting Seasons

Hunting is allowed in the National Forest and Missouri Department of Conservation areas that the OT travels through. Check with the Missouri Department of Conservation for a list of Hunting Season dates.

## Weather

Dress appropriately. Cotton fabrics hold moisture and do not breathe. Wear breathable clothing. Any good outdoor clothing store will be able to outfit you. Wear enough clothes. Don't risk being too cold in cold weather. Even in warm weather, be prepared for cool fronts. Thunderstorms often move in quickly, bring colder air, and soak you to the bone. If you're on an extended hike, pack rain gear, and have dry clothes to change into.

## Dehydration

Even in winter, it is very possible to become dehydrated. Dehydration may cause light-headedness, nausea, vomiting, or a headache. Prolonged dehydration can become extremely dangerous, with possible loss of consciousness and shock. Pack more water than you think you'll need. Carry a water purifier or water purifying tablets if you can't carry all the water that you will need. All water for cooking and drinking should be treated first. A few sections have little to no water and many creeks and springs go dry in seasons with little rain or snow.

## Rising water after rains

The OT crosses a lot of creeks and a few major rivers. Not many of these crossings have bridges. Spring can be a very wet time of the year, and anytime of the year heavy rains can occur and create flooding conditions. Even if it isn't raining, but may have rained a day earlier, many run-off creeks can rise very quickly – as much as 10' in an hour! Do not attempt to cross swift moving creeks. Flooding conditions are dangerous and life threatening.

## Poison ivy

There is a lot of poison ivy in Missouri. Wear a long sleeve shirt and long pants to help prevent from getting the poison ivy oils on your skin. Wash immediately after exposure. A good scrub in a creek or river with mud can help to minimize a reaction.

## Ticks /chiggers

Use bug spray, especially on shoes, ankles, outer clothing. Sometimes they ignore bug spray, so be sure to check yourself thoroughly for ticks after possible exposure.

## Dogs

Over the entire 350 miles we encountered two dogs that weren't with people. Neither one attacked, but both were intimidating. Have a plan of defense.

## Snakes

Although we saw a handful of snakes as we covered the trail, none were venomous. There ARE venomous snakes throughout the Ozarks.

Copperheads and Rattlesnakes will deliver a dangerous bite, especially when startled. So keep your eyes open for them, especially around sun-drenched rocks. Keep your distance.

## Trailside Camping

Camping is permitted on U.S. Forest Service and Department of Natural Resources land 100 feet from the trail and 100 feet from water sources. Do not camp in glade areas. Camping is not permitted trailside on Missouri Department of Conservation lands. The building of rock fire rings is not permitted. The practice of leaving your campsite so that no one can tell you were there is encouraged.

# The Ozark Trail Association

## Volunteering and building the Ozark Trail

As the Ozark Trail approached its 25th anniversary, several trail enthusiasts began discussing ways to push the original 1977 trail concept to completion. As they looked at other successful trail systems around the country, they realized the Ozark Trail was missing something the others shared— a strong volunteer organization. In March of 2002, they made a pitch to the trail's coordinating group, the Ozark Trail Council— why don't we look into creating our own volunteer non-profit organization?

The council agreed. That summer, John Donjoian & John Roth researched the issue. They surveyed other trail systems, solicited volunteer groups for advice, posted to message groups and emailed interested parties. On October 26th, they made their pitch to the Council— volunteer groups are a key to a trail's success, and we want to start one for the Ozark Trail. The Ozark Trail Council unanimously backed the idea.

On November 13th, 2002 the Ozark Trail Association took its first baby steps. 27 people met to lay the groundwork of a new volunteer non-profit, and agreed that: *The Mission of the Ozark Trail Association is to **develop**, **maintain**, **preserve**, **promote** and **protect** the rugged, natural beauty of the Ozark Trail.*

We're a small group today, and we've got a lot of work ahead to make this a successful organization. We'll undoubtedly experience some growing pains. The OTA needs your input, your help and your patience. You are invited to join the Ozark Trail Association. Write to the address below or visit the website. New members receive a members packet, an OTA patch, and a quarterly newsletter. Most of all, you'll receive the satisfaction of helping the Trail become one of the gems of the Ozarks.

Ozark Trail Association

483 S. Kirkwood Road #40

Kirkwood, MO 63122

**www.ozarktrail.com**

Kansas City

St. Louis

Leasburg

Courtois Creek Section

Trace Creek Section

Middle Fork Section

Taum Sauk Section

Karkaghne Section

Marble Creek Section

Blair Creek Section

Wappapello Lake Section

Current River Section

Springfield

Between the Rivers Section

North Fork Section

Eleven Point River Section

Victory Section

Poplar Bluff

# The Ozark Trail

# Ozark Trail Sections

| Section | Miles | Notes |
|---|---|---|
| St. Louis Area | ---- | Planning stages |
| Meramec River | ---- | Pre-planning stages |
| Courtois Creek | 37.69 | Scenic bluffs |
| Trace Creek | 23.79 | Creeks and caves |
| Middle Fork | 25.00 | Under construction |
| Karkaghne | 25.64 | River bluffs, Grasshopper Hollow |
| Blair Creek | 25.10 | Wildflowers, springs, river views |
| Current River | 30.00 | Rocky Creek, Stegall Mountain |
| Between the Rivers | 24.21 | Wooded hillsides |
| Eleven Point River | 25.88 | River views, springs, wildflowers |
| North Fork River | 26.68 | River views, wooded hillsides |
| Taum Sauk | 32.85 | Mountain top views, glades |
| Marble Creek | 8.25 | Crane Lake, wooded hillsides |
| St. Francis River | ---- | Pre-planning stages |
| Wappapello Lake | 30.91 | Wooded hillsides |
| Victory | 22.69 | Wooded hillsides, creeks |

# MAP LEGEND

—————  Ozark Trail

🐎  Equestrians Allowed

🚶  Foot Traffic Allowed

🚲  Mountain Bicycles Allowed

TH  Trailhead and Parking Area

★  Scenic Location

⛺  Campground

▲  Trail Camping Location

—⬯E⬯—  Paved Road

—————  Gravel or dirt road

—————  River

—————  Creek

Body of water

6.50 mile  Trail Mileage

●  City / Town

⋯⋯⋯  Powercut / Pipeline

# The Ozark Trail

The OT logo is a registered mark of the Ozark Trail Council.

Patti Welch enjoys an early spring hike along the
river bluffs of the Courtois Creek.

# COURTOIS CREEK
## Section

DISTANCE 37.69 miles
TRAIL USERS foot, bike, horse
Only FOOT TRAFFIC in the Huzzah Conservation Area

## ABOUT THIS SECTION

Pronounced "code-a-way", this section is currently the northern most part of the Ozark Trail, beginning in the Huzzah Conservation area just across the Meramec River from Onondaga State Park, and a little over an hour away from the St. Louis County line. The section of trail that travels through the Huzzah Conservation Area is restricted to foot traffic only.

This section travels past scenic bluffs, caves, springs, savannahs, pine trees and an interesting area called the "Narrows". The trail travels through the Huzzah Conservation area that was once home to the Scotia Furnace and Iron Works. Remains of the furnace, which produced pig iron from 1870 to 1880 and wonderful river bluffs can be found along the trail. Before leaving the Huzzah Conservation Area the trail travels through the "Narrows", which is an area on a ridge separating the Huzzah and Courtois Creeks.

This section of the Ozark Trail is not complete yet, so after passing through the Huzzah Conservation area, you can get to the next part of the trail by traveling about 5 miles on roads that are mostly gravel. Then the trail returns to the woods and on to the Berryman trail and the Mark Twain National Forest. The Berryman area is very popular with equestrians and mountain bike riders. It

USGS Quadrangle maps:
Onondaga Cave,
Huzzah, Berryman,
Courtois

CAMPING FACILITIES
Camping is permitted
along the trail in USFS
lands 100' from the trail.

Huzzah
Conservation Area-
primitive, pit toilets, fire
rings.

Berryman Recreation
Area- primitive, pit toilets,
tables, fire rings.

Hazel Creek Recreation
Area- primitive, pit toilets,
tables, fire rings.

Onondaga State Park-
camping, showers, water,
store.

NEAREST TOWNS &
SERVICES
Leasburg, Steelville and
Potosi

Ozark Outdoors
Store, camping cabins,
shuttle service
1-800-888-0023
www.ozarkoutdoors.net

Bass Resort
Store, camping cabins
1-800-392-3700
www.bassresort.com

was also home to a Civilian Conservation Crew in the 1930's. Remnants of some of the buildings can be found at the Berryman Recreation Area. The trail heads on to the Hazel Creek Recreation Area where the Courtois Creek Section ends and the Trace Creek Section begins.

Even though this section of the Ozark Trail is relatively close to one of the largest cities in the Midwest the traveler will find a lot of wilderness and may not encounter any other trail travelers. Creek crossings, river bluffs, savannahs, stands of pine trees all await you. Camping in Huzzah Conservation Area is only permitted in the established campground.

There is a store at Onondaga State Park and at Ozark Outdoors canoe outfitter located off Highway H. Both have a limited selection of groceries and other items. Ozark Outdoors also has cabins, camping and offers a trail shuttle service. While on the section of trail on the road you will pass Bass' canoe outfitter which also has a store, cabins and camping.

## HOW TO GET THERE:
### Trailhead Parking areas
**Huzzah Conservation Area North Trailhead-Northern terminus-** (7 miles from Interstate 44) From Leasburg and I-44 take State Highway H south towards Onondaga State Park. Cross the Meramec River Bridge and a small parking area is located on the left.

**Huzzah Conservation Area South access-** From Leasburg and I-44 take State Highway H east towards Onondaga

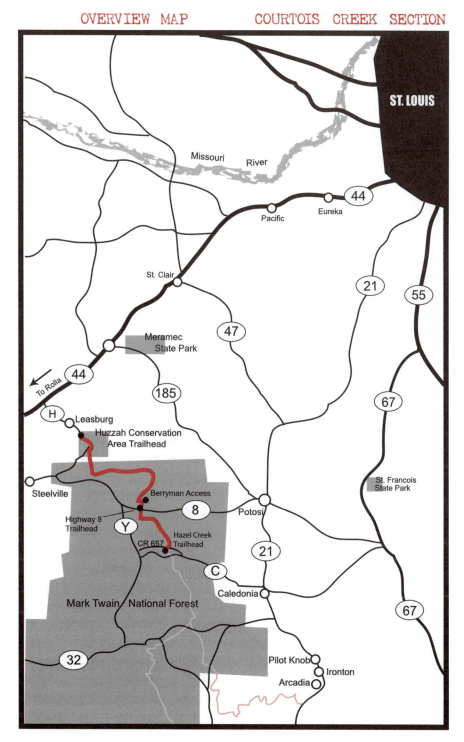

State Park. Cross the Meramec River Bridge and continue past the first trailhead small parking area on the left. Continue straight on this road. Turn left at road marked for the shooting range, but continue straight. The road will come to a campground. Loop around to the parking area at the Courtois Creek.

**Berryman Recreation Area/Mark Twain National Forest Trailhead-**Located north of hwy 8 between Steelville and Potosi on Forest Road 2266 (Shirley Ridge Road). Watch for the Mark Twain National Forest sign on hwy 8 marking this turn. The trailhead is located about 1.5 miles from hwy 8.

**Mark Twain National Forest Highway 8 Trailhead-** On hwy 8 between Potosi and Steelville. At the time of publishing the trailhead consists of an old white house and a small field that is being used for parking, there is one small sign. There are trail markers showing the trail coming down from the hillside, crossing Highway 8 and continuing on the west side of the fence line.

**Hazel Creek Recreation Area/Mark Twain National Forest Trailhead-Southern terminus-** From the intersection of Highways 8 and Y, go south on Y for approximately 7 miles then make a left on County Road 657. Take CR 657 west approximately 1.3 miles. Watch for a sign for Hazel Creek Recreational Area. From the sign, turn on to the gravel road for about 1 mile.

## Possible Day Trips
Huzzah north trailhead to Huzzah south trailhead (one-way) 6.59 miles.

Berryman Campgroung to Hazel Creek Campground (one-way) 13 miles.

## Contacts
Missouri Department of Conservation
P.O. Box 180
Jefferson City, MO 65102
573-468-5427

US Forest Service-
Postosi District
Highway 8 West
Potosi, MO 63664
573-468-5427

## Trail Description North to South

The Ozark Trail through the Huzzah Conservation area is limited to foot traffic only. The remaining miles of the Courtois section allow foot, bike and horse users. This section begins at the Huzzah north Trailhead on State Highway H, just south of the Meramec River Bridge at the entrance to the Huzzah Conservation Area. A small parking area for two vehicles is located on Highway H. The start of the trail enters the woods across the road from the parking area by the Huzzah Conservation Area sign. The trail parallels Highway H and a dry creek bed on a gradual uphill. Pass a small wildlife pond on the left, and then the trail crosses a small dirt/grass service road. Continue up the slope in the woods to a metal bridge that crosses the creek bed (.58 mile / 38.02.993N, 91.12.989W). The trail turns eastward and crosses State Highway H and continues uphill to the top of the ridge. This is a fairly steep ascent, with several switchbacks to ease the climb. Travel along the ridge top and the trail follows a gravel road which splits. Stay to the right. There are several benches and wildlife food plots along this part of the trail. This is a designated wildlife viewing area. Go past the metal gate (1.72 mile / 38.02.540N, 91.12.226W) and cross the gravel road, Scotia Ranch Road.

After crossing Scotia Ranch road the trail returns to the forest. At the fork stay to the left (the trail to the right just leads to the gravel road H). The trail leads to a food plot clearing with a bench, go straight across and re-enter the woods. Continue on past a pond and to a clearing with a small bluff. This is a nice wildflower area. The trail turns to the left and climbs up above the small bluff. The trail comes to a wider two-track dirt road turn right here and follow the road through the pines.

After a gradual climb, the trail changes to singletrack. The trail gradually makes its way down to the Courtois Creek, and along the bluffs. This is a beautiful area, with views of the creek, bluffs, caves and interesting rock formations. This area is especially pleasant in the Fall during peak color. After leaving the bluff area along the creek, the trail enters a small clearing, that serves as the Huzzah south parking area (4.41 mile / 38.01.403N, 91.11.972W). The trail continues on the road a short distance through the campground (this may be changed as a reroute is being discussed). Watch for trail markers.

The trail returns to the forest on the left side of the campground road. Follow the trail back to the Courtois Creek. This area also has scenic bluffs. Cross the creek (4.70 mile / 38.01.305N, 91.12.185W), and expect this to be a wet crossing, with mid calf to deaper water. As with any water crossing do not attempt to cross when at dangerous levels. After the crossing, the trail travels up close to the bluffs and past Bat Cave. The cave has a gated entrance to allow the resident bats an undisturbed habitat. The trail climbs up above the bluffs and continues along a ridgeline through "the Narrrows". This "hogback" ridge separates the Courtois and Huzzah Creeks' watersheds.

Travel along the top of the ridge for a while before descending to the boundary of the Huzzah Conservation Area. At the time of publication the trail from this point to Butts Road was so overgrown it could not be followed. The route is shown on the map as a dashed line. Hopefully in the near future this section of trail will be adopted and maintained. Until that time there is a gravel road that can be followed to Butts Road.

Currently there is a gap here in the trail until some land purchases can be made, so there is no official Ozark Trail for the next 4.17 miles. For those willing and looking to "thru hike" this section, continue on by turning left on Butts Road (8.81 mile / 37.58.709N, 91.10.957W). The paved road will take you past Bass'

Resort and a low water bridge across the Courtois Creek (10.37 mile / 37.59.527N, 91.09.909W). Bass' Resort has a store, cabins and camping facilities. After the bridge, the road turns to gravel and heads up hill, stay on this road (FR 2265) for 2.43 miles.

The OT will cut into the woods on the right side (12.80 mile / 37.59.098N, 91.07.527W). This spot is only marked with the green and white Ozark Trail markers. The trail travels in the woods and parallels the road. Cross FR 2757 and then FR 2265. Then cross gravel road, FR 2265 (13.72 mile / 37.58.883N, 91.06.536W), and the trail traverses the oak and hickory forest through Henpeck Hollow. Cross FR 2284 and then continue on to Harmon Spring where it joins the Berryman Trail. The Berryman Trail is a 24-mile loop trail that is very popular with mountain bike riders and equestrians.

Shortly after passing Harmon Spring the trail begins to travel in a southern direction, and crosses FR 2265 ( 19.14 mile / 37.58.815N, 91.02.797W). The trail passes the Artesian well spring. Be sure to treat all water before drinking. Continue to the junction (25.21 mile) of the spur trail to the Berryman Recreation Area. To get to the primitive campground continue straight on the Berryman trail for .3 miles. From this junction the Hazel Creek Recreation area is 14.5 miles.

Continue on the Ozark Trail, and the trail begins a downhill trek to Highway 8 (26.42 mile / 37.55.039N, 91.04.560W). Highway 8 is a major paved high speed highway. Cross Highway 8 and the trail goes back into the woods just west of the crossing, watch for markers along the fence. It is a short walk to Lost Creek, which should have water most of the year. After the crossing, the trail cuts up into woods and begins the climb out of the valley. The trail works its way to FR 2591. After crossing, a downhill begins through pines, oaks and hickories to a dry creek crossing. The next road crossing is CR 602 (28.06 mile / 37.53.814N, 91.04.701W). The trail gets fairly level. Make two dry creek crossings then cross FR 2541A into Machell Hollow.

In Machell Hollow there are two creek crossings. These are unreliable water sources. Then cross CR 603, which is also called FR 2247(30.02 mile / 37.53.872N, 91.02.946W). The trail travels through the forest on the east side of CR 603/ FR 2247 for .9 miles, crossing a dry creek and an old forest road (now closed

NORTH
one mile
scale: 5/8" = 1 mile

Brazil Creek Campground

FR 2266

Brazil Creek

Little Brazil Creek

Edward Beecher Artesian Well Spring

FR 2265

19.14 mile

Harmon Spring Trail Camp

FR 2284

CR 205

W

N

Henpeck Hollow

13.72 mile

CR 519

FR 2265

12.80 mile

Off Road and Back to trail

On Road

Bass Canoe Outfitters

10.37 mile

CR 552

Meramec River

Ozark Outdoors

Huzzah Conservation Area Trailhead

Gate & Parking Area

1.72 mile

Scotia Ranch Rd

WOW spot Bluffs along the Courtois Creek

Courtois Creek

CR 550

8.81 mile

Huzzah Creek

8

Onondaga State Park

To Leasburg

H

TH

CR 537

Huzzah Conservation Area Campground

4.41 mile

Bat Cave

The Narrows

To Steelville

To Potosi

8

Little Lost Creek

FR 2767

34.91 mile

Palmer

FR 2698

Snapps Branch

Town Branch

FR 2247/ CR 603

30.86 mile

Boiling Springs Hollow

FR 2266

Shirley Ridge Road

FR 2267

Berryman Trailhead Campground

TH

Blips Branch

Lost Creek

CR 602

Machell Hollow

FR 2099

FR 2514

FR 2240

FR 2541A

Hazel Creek

Hazel Creek Campground/Trailhead

37.69 mile

TH

Highway 8 Trailhead

26.42 mile

TH

28.06 mile

Courtois Creek

CR 657

Y

Huzzah Creek

The bluffs at the crossing of the Courtois Creek.

with no #), and then crosses CR 603 again (30.86 mile / 37.53.509N, 91.02.487W). After crossing, continue on and cross a creek then FR 2514 (31.99 mile). Shortly after that, cross FR 2240 (32.16 mile). Years ago this area was very popular with miners. Keep your eyes open for "pits" located along the trail from here to Hazel Creek. Miners looking for minerals created these "pit mines". The next road crossing is FR 2099 (32.97 mile / 37.52.463N, 91.01.528W) and then a double track dirt road (no #, closed).

At the edge of Boiling Springs Hollow the trail crosses a creek bed and continues to a place where the trail turns right and a small trail goes off to the left, go right here. The trail travels through the lowland bottom area before heading back uphill with some switchbacks. Between here and the crossing of FR 2698 there are more "pit mines" along the trail. After crossing FR 2698, in about a mile you will come to some switchbacks going down hill. Cross a dirt road and then you will come to a wet creek crossing at Snapps Branch (34.91 mile / 37.51.393N, 91.00.570W). (Usually in the Ozarks when the word branch is used it refers to the water that connects a spring to a creek or larger body of water).

From Snapps Branch, it's up some switch backs and a pretty good climb to the top of the ridge. The descent down is pretty steep with some loose corners. Cross a small creek. Just past the creek is a small seep spring with watercress and moss. When you get to FR 2767 there is a four way crossing. The Ozark Trail turns to the left. In a short distance the trail returns to the woods on the left. Within a quarter of a mile the trail will follow a creek.

Cross a scenic ravine that turns into a rock-lined drop into the creek lined with ferns. The creek will be on the left. Cross another ravine that leads to the creek, then follow to an area with lots of tall grasses and some pine trees. From here, the trail heads uphill and has some water bars across it for the next .4 mile before crossing an old road (no #, closed). Cross two more old closed roads. The trail then goes up and down some small hills and crosses a well-traveled gravel road FR 2540 (37.17 mi / 37.50.610N, 91.00.620W). The trail enters an area with some nice single track along the side of a ridge, then crosses another well-traveled gravel road CR 657 (37.49 mi / 37.50.429N, 91.00.845W). In just a short distance you will come to another gravel road.

## COURTOIS CREEK SECTION

This is Hazel Creek Recreation Area (37.69 mile). Go right down the gravel road FR 2392. Just .03 miles down the road is the southern terminus of the Courtois Creek and the beginning of the Trace Creek Section. A bit father down the gravel road is the camping area.

# Trail Notes

The crossing at Trace Creek.

# TRACE CREEK
## Section

DISTANCE 23.79 MILES
TRAIL USERS foot, bike, horse

## ABOUT THIS SECTION

This section travels past springs, crosses several creeks, and goes through a savannah. A spur trail about 13 miles from the start leads to Council Bluff Lake Recreation Area and Campground. Just south of the Council Bluff spur, hikers will see the cut-off to the new Middle Fork Section, which is currently under construction and is scheduled to be completed late 2005. When completed, the Middle Fork Section will lead to the northern terminus of the Karkaghne Section, and hikers will be able to enjoy a 211-mile through-hike. The Trace Creek section continues on to the southern terminus at Highway A and the Bell Mountain Wilderness Trailhead.

## HOW TO GET THERE: Trailhead Parking areas

**Hazel Creek Recreation Area Trailhead-** Located south of Highway 8, between Steelville and Potosi. From Highway 8 turn south on Highway Y. Go approximately 7.5 miles and turn left on County Road 657. Take CR 657 about 1.3 miles, watch for the Hazel Creek Recreational Area sign. From the sign, turn on the gravel road, about 1 mile to the parking area.

**Bell Mountain Wilderness/Highway A Trailhead-** Located south of Potosi on Highway A. From Potosi take Highway 21 south to Highway 32. Turn right (west) on Highway 32, turn left (south) on

Highway A. Watch for the Bell Mountain Wilderness sign and the trailhead parking area is on the right (west) side.

## Trail Description North to South

Leaving the Hazel Creek Recreation Area you will find the trail on the south side of FR 2392, just east of the campground. The trail heads up to a ridge that has some very large pine trees. Some are so large you won't be able to get your arms around them. Make your way through a grassy area and to a road that ATVs travel. This area gets over grown and the trail marker in the field gets knocked down occasionally. The trail returns to the woods and then to a clearing with power lines and a small creek. The creek is Town Branch (.59 mile / 37.50.180N, 91.00.350W). Use caution, as this creek can get quite a bit of water in it, and the bank is steep. Head uphill into some pine trees. The trail levels out with a few ups and downs, then crosses a dirt road. The trail climbs again through a nice grove of pine trees. As you get closer to Hazel Creek the area is getting illegal ATV use and it gets confusing with the ATV paths criss-crossing over the Ozark Trail. Pay attention for the next mile to stay on the trail and not follow an ATV path. Hazel Creek is one of the larger creek crossings on the Ozark Trail. It is considered a major permanently flowing creek (1.20 mile / 37.49.669N, 91.00.370W). The beavers like to build dams across the creek in this area.

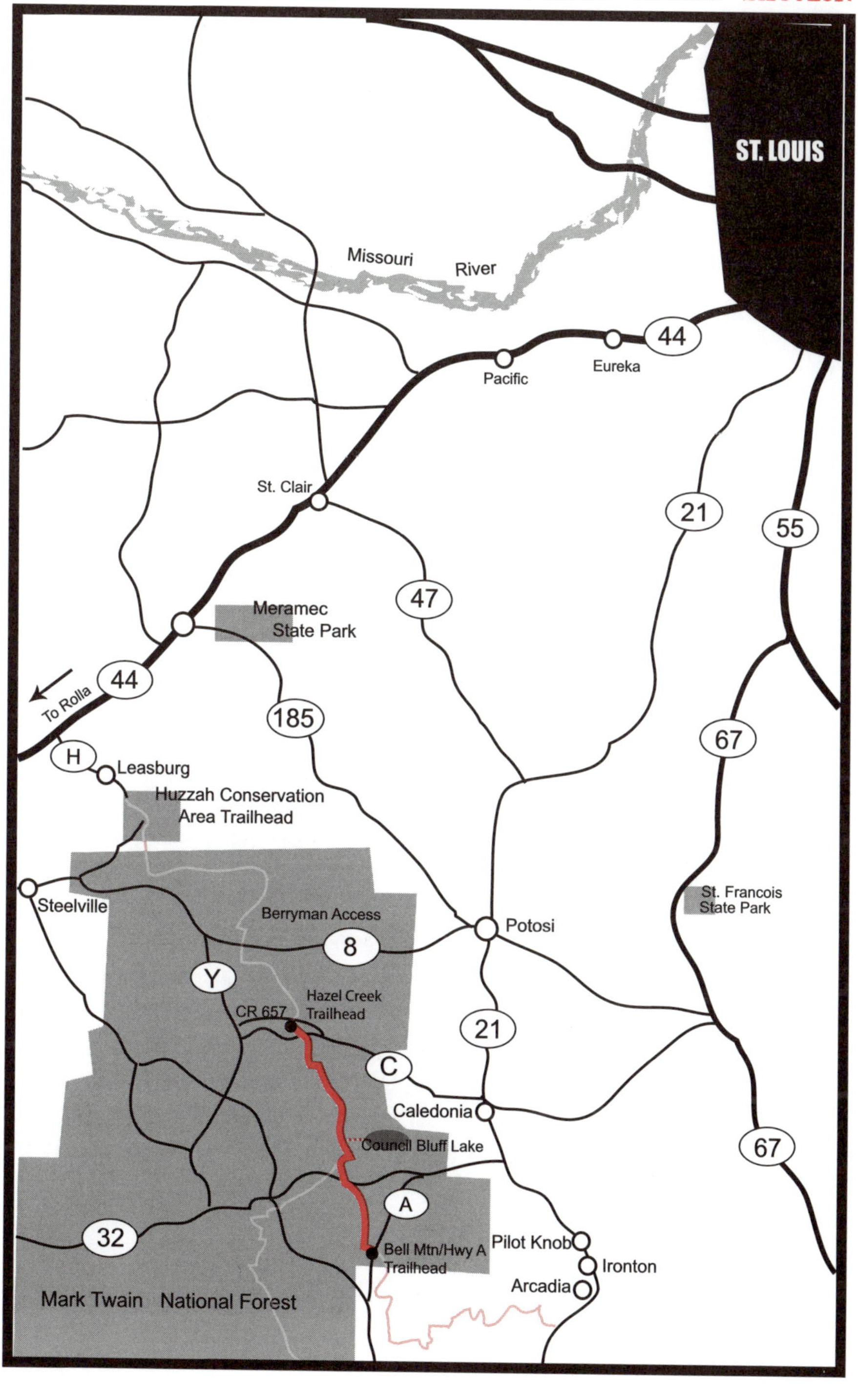

ST. LOUIS

Missouri     River

44

Pacific    Eureka

21    55

St. Clair

47

Meramec
State Park

44

To Rolla    185

H    67

Leasburg
Huzzah Conservation
Area Trailhead

Steelville

Berryman Access    Potosi

8    St. Francois
State Park

Y

Hazel Creek
CR 657    Trailhead

C

21

Caledonia

Council Bluff Lake    67

A

32    Bell Mtn/Hwy A    Pilot Knob
Trailhead

Ironton

Arcadia

Mark Twain   National Forest

Possible Day Hikes
Highway 32/ DD
Trailhead to the Highway
A-Bell Mountain
Trailhead (one-way) 9.5
miles.

Highway 32/ DD
Trailhead to Council Bluff
Lake Recreation Area
Campground (one-way) 3
miles.

Contacts
US Forest Service-
Postosi District
Highway 8 West
Potosi, MO 63664
573-468-5427

Cross the creek. The trail parallels the creek on it's southern side in the valley on a wider trail that gets some ATV use. A dirt road comes in on the right. The trail stays to the left, still paralleling the creek. The wide trail will begin to climb uphill, changing into singletrack in the trees. Just about at the top of the hill the trail is wide again. Along this climb, listen for the creek below and watch for views of it between the trees. Head down hill. The trail crosses a dirt road with no number then goes through a little clearing that gets overgrown from time to time with briars. This area also gets some ATV use. Continue on the trail and it gets relatively flat and crosses a creek bed. Cross FR 2913 and two more creek beds, then the trail goes uphill. Cross over some big flat rocks that lay in the trail. The trail is wider in here. This part of the trail was scarcely marked for about the next mile. Cross another no-number dirt road. The next few tenths of a mile is fairly level near the top of the ridge (2.90 mile). This is a nice area. The trail goes uphill a bit to some neat rocks on the right side and then to more neat rocks (3.29 mile / 37.48.600N, 90.59.822W). The trail begins its descent from here to the Little Piney Branch, which might have water (3.78 mile / 37.48.398N, 90.59.479W).

The next .65 mile is an ascent to the State Highway C road crossing (4.43 mile / 37.47.964N, 90.59.158W). The trail resumes on the other side of the highway and heads downhill to a small creek crossing. This creek is not a reliable source for water. At the 4.93 mile point there is a stand of pine trees and the trail continues in a southerly direction past two dirt road crossings (5.52 mile, 5.66 mile). Neither have numbers.

After crossing Delbridge Ridge Road (also known as FR2250 or County Road 646), it's a fairly level walk for about a half-mile, until the trail begins downhill. At the bottom of the hill, just where the trail joins with a forest road, there was a large pile of cut cedars on the trail that may need to be skirted. There is an old chimney visible from here. The trail traces forest roads through here; to the right, or south from the chimney, then to the left for a short distance, then to the right and back into the woods. Watch for markers!  Follow the trail to the crossing of Trace Creek (7.07 mile, 37.46.653N, 90.58.113W). It looks as though there would be water year-around. The creek may get quite swollen during rains. It can also be easily stone-stepped across under dryer conditions.

From here follow an arm of the creek and cross it twice before climbing to the top of the ridge at dirt road CR 648 (1304) (8.87 mile / 37.45.539N, 90.56.998W). The next major road, State Highway DD crossing is 3.5 miles. From CR 648 the trail heads downhill, goes back up to the top of another hill, heads downhill to a nice stand of pine trees (9.46 mile, 37.45.094N, 90.57.117W). The trail continues down some switchbacks to a creek crossing (9.85 mile / 37.44.915N, 90.57.257W) which can have a good amount of water in it, but may also dry up in dry months. The trail will cross back over the creek again in this flat area and will start up a pretty good climb with some switchbacks. At the top of the hill there is an old forest road (10.55 mile / 37.44.587N, 90.57.056W). Head downhill through some switchback sections to a shallow creek crossing (11.01 mile / 37.44.424N, 90.57.330W). At the crossing, notice the cane growing. The trail starts going up with the creek on the right side to another crossing, then passes a round seep spring with bamboo/cane growing around it. The seep doesn't have much of a flow to it. (11.25 mile / 37.44.235N, 90.57.262W). The trail bends to the right and heads uphill through some switchbacks to an old closed forest road crossing (11.54 mile / 37.44.109N, 90.57.308W). Continue uphill and cross another old closed forest road crossing (11.67 mile / 37.43.994N, 90.57.316W). From here there are some small ups and downs to a crossing of an old forest road (11.95 mile / 37.43.816N,

An old chimney along the trail near Delbridge.

90.57.170W) then to the crossing of paved state road DD (12.18 mile / 37.43.663N, 90.57.192W). The next paved road crossing is 5.58 miles at State Road 32.

From DD the trail begins a descent for the next 1.25 miles through some switchbacks to a small creek (12.40 mile / 37.43.509N, 90.57.053W). It might have some pools most of the year, that may dry up in the summer. The trail will follow this small creek, crossing it again three times, and then lead a spring (12.84 mile / 37.43.203N, 90.56.847W). Near the spring is an area that is used to camp. In early spring the spring peepers can be very loud here. After leaving the spring area stay on the wide part of the trail. It may be marked with silver diamonds. There are pines on the left, and a creek on the right. Then there is another creek bed crossing that flows into the bigger creek. The creek bed is still on the right, pines on the left, and the trail is flat. Soon the trail crosses the creek bed. There is an area to camp on the other side of the creek (13.26 mile / 37.43.101N, 90.56.414W). The trail is still down in the flats. In a short distance, cross the creek again. Next you will come to the junction with the spur trail that goes to the left to Council Bluff Lake Recreation Area (13.39 mile / 37.43.083N, 90.56.274W). It's about .5 miles to the lake and a little further to the campground. Continue to the right on the Ozark Trail. The creek that the trail has been following comes to a "Y" where another creek flows in. The trail follows the new creek which is the Telleck Branch. The trail is smaller single track here and begins a gradual ascent. The trail comes to a creek crossing. There it goes between two creeks, and climbs up on a ridge. This is quite a neat area where the ridge is moss covered (13.77 mile, 37.42.867N, 90.56.547W).

In a little less than a tenth of a mile watch for a beautiful little spring that comes out of the side of the hill and the bright green of the watercress growing in it (13.85 mile, 37.42.838N, 90.56.591W). After the spring, the trail goes uphill. The trail continues up and gets rockier for the next half a mile to switchbacks (14.36 mile, 37.42.657N, 90.57.081W). Continue climbing to a crossing of an old dirt road (14.64 mile, 37.42.533N, 90.57.240W). This dirt road does not show on the current USGS maps.

The trail begins its descent to the head waters of the Big River. The trail leads to a power cut (15.20 mile, 37.42.135N,

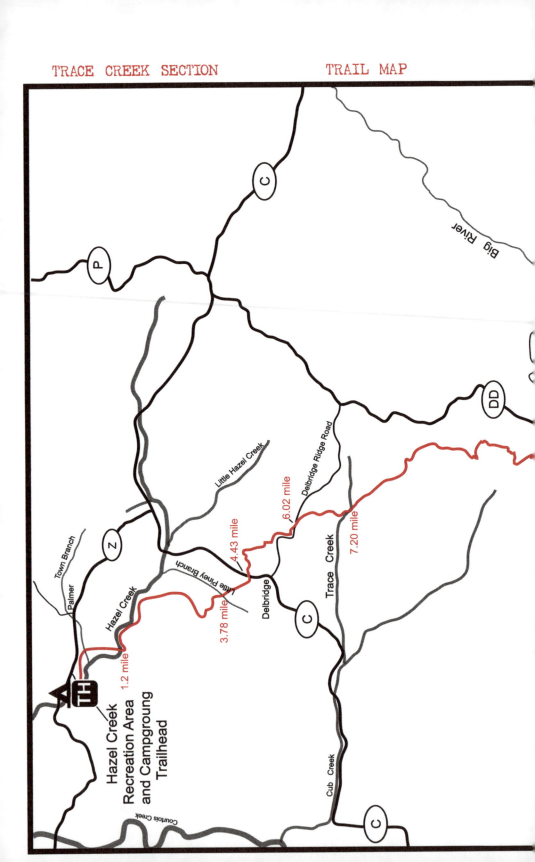

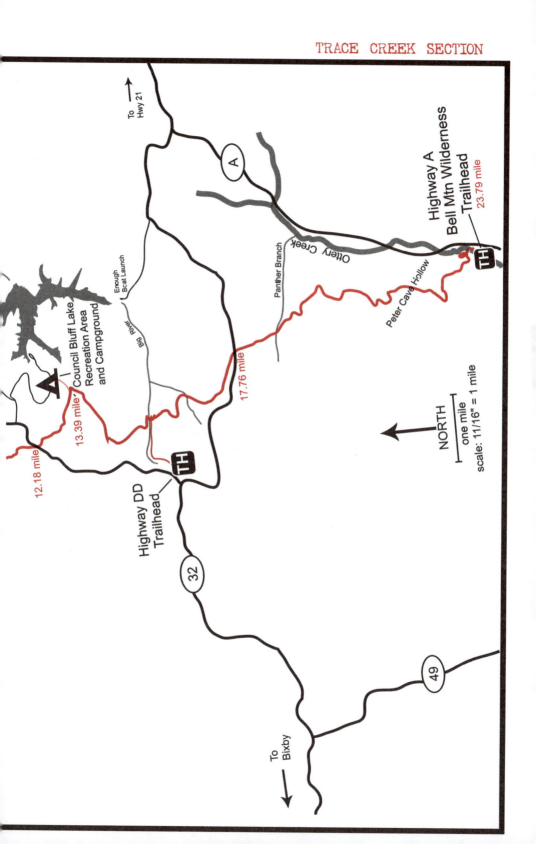

To Hwy 21

A

Highway A
Bell Mtn Wilderness
Trailhead
23.79 mile

Ottery Creek

Panther Branch

Peter Cave Hollow

Enough
Boat Launch

Big River

Council Bluff Lake
Recreation Area
and Campground

17.76 mile

13.39 mile

12.18 mile

NORTH

one mile
scale: 11/16" = 1 mile

TH

Highway DD
Trailhead

32

49

To
Bixby

The spring at the 13.85 mile point.

90.57.046W). Go left. Follow the power cut and the trail cuts to the right into the woods. There has been some discussion that this section of trail may be re-routed to avoid the seep area. Just after entering the woods the trail is at a beautiful creek with a little clearing after the creek. There is an area used to camp. The new Middle Fork Section spur trail comes in here from the right.

Continue on the Trace Creek Section uphill into pine trees, and through some switchbacks. Then begin downhill through switchbacks to the bottom land forest. Sections of the trail along here are moss covered and very pretty. The trail begins its uphill climb towards Highway 32. You'll be able to hear and see traffic on the road after crossing a small dirt road that doesn't show on the USGS maps. After paralleling the highway for a short distance you come to the crossing of the paved road, State Highway 32 (17.76 mile, 37.40.866N, 90.55.942W). It's now just 6.03 miles to the southern terminus at Bell Mountain.

From Highway 32 it's a steady down hill to a dry creek bed. Follow to a creek, Panther Branch, that probably has water in it most of the time. The creek is about six feet across and you can cross without getting your feet wet, in low water conditions. The creek loops around and the trail crosses again. It is level through here. The trail crosses the creek again (18.66 mile / 37.40.171N, 90.55.611W) and it is wider and sandy here, with some signs of ATV use in this area.

The trail heads uphill. At the top of the hill, the trail follows a wide forest road to the left. After a short distance, the OT turns off of the forest road. The trail is clearly marked. The trail follows a ridge, and then descends to a creek crossing. The creek is usually dry with a few puddles. The trail heads uphill again. At the top, the trail follows a forest road to the left for about .4 miles, and then cuts back into the woods to the right. The trail winds along the hillside and eventually leads down into Peter Cave Hollow. In the hollow, cross a forest road to another creek, which had about a foot of water, small fish in it, and is about 10' across (21.7 mile / 37.38.457N, 90.55.179W). From here, it's just over two miles to the Highway A Trailhead.

After crossing the creek, the trail follows through a small grove of cedars and short grasses. The trail heads uphill from about 1000 feet in elevation, to over 1200' in the next .7 miles.

## TRACE CREEK SECTION

Near the top, the trail joins a forest road to the left. This is very easy going, and is pretty up here. After .65 miles, the OT leaves the forest road to the left. This area can be overgrown with briars. After a short distance, the trail goes down switchbacks to Ottery Creek. This will most likely be a wet crossing, and may be dangerous or impassable in wet weather. After the creek, it's just a short distance to the Highway A Trailhead (23.79 mile / 37.37.514N, 90.54.675W). This is the southern terminus of the Trace Creek Section of the Ozark Trail.

# Trail Notes

_____

_____

_____

_____

_____

_____

_____

_____

_____

_____

_____

_____

_____

_____

_____

_____

_____

_____

_____

_____

_____

_____

_____

_____

_____

_____

_____

_____

_____

_____

_____

Volunteers gather at one of the "Mega Events" to build the Middle Fork Section of the Ozark Trail. For more information on volunteering visit www.ozarktrail.com

# MIDDLE FORK
## Section

DISTANCE approximately 25 miles
TRAIL USERS foot, bike, horse

## ABOUT THIS SECTION

The Middle Fork Section is the newest section of the Ozark Trail.  Construction began in 2002 and continues today with the help of many volunteers.  This section is completed from the Highway DD Trailhead, north to the connection with the Trace Creek Section, and south past Neals Creek.  This section travels through scenic wooded Ozark hills past several creek crossings and near a fen.

Currently over twelve miles of the total 25 miles have been built.  When completed, the Middle Fork Section will connect the Trace Creek Section to the Karkaghne Section, and then nearly 210 miles of continuous trail will be available.  This will make for an outstanding long distance trail experience.

Volunteers are needed for many tasks, and if you would like to get involved visit the Ozark Trail Association website for volunteer information, www.ozarktrail.com.

## HOW TO GET THERE: Trailhead Parking areas

**Highway DD Trailhead-** Located on Highway DD, just north of the intersection with Highway 32.  From Highway 21 south of Caledonia, turn west on Highway 32.  Go 15 miles and turn right (north) on Highway DD.  The Trailhead is located on the right.  Currently this is the only trailhead on this section.

MAPS
USGS Quadrangle maps:
Johnson Mtn, Viburnum
East, Oates.


CAMPING FACILITIES
Camping is permitted
along the trail in USFS
lands 100' from the trail.



NEAREST TOWNS &
SERVICES
Bixby, Viburnum, Potosi.

## Trail Description North to South

This section begins at the Highway DD Trailhead and the trail leads both north and south from here. To the north the trail travels 1.35 miles to the intersection with the Trace Creek Section. To the south the Middle Fork Section travels approximately 24 miles to Highway J and the northern terminus of the Karkaghne Section. At publication time, this section has been completed from the intersection with the Trace Creek Section south to near Neals Creek. From the Highway DD Trailhead the trail travels south nearly a mile to the crossing of Highway 32. This is a paved high-speed roadway, cross with care. Continue 2.4 miles along the headwaters of the Middle Fork of the Black River to the crossing of County Road 72. Traverse nearly 3.5 miles to Wolfpen Hollow and then nearly 1.5 miles to the crossing of County Road 73. As of publication time this is where the completed trail ends.

When construction is finished, the Middle Fork Section will continue across County Road 73 and cross Brooks Creek. Then the trail will travel about .7 miles to Highway 49. This is a paved high-speed roadway, cross with care. Next the trail will descend approximately 1.3 miles to Henderson Creek. Cross the creek and the trail will climb nearly a mile out of the valley. The trail will continue 1.25 miles to the crossing of County Road 79.

The trail will continue about a tenth of a mile to the crossing of Neals Creek, and then climb partially up the ridge. It

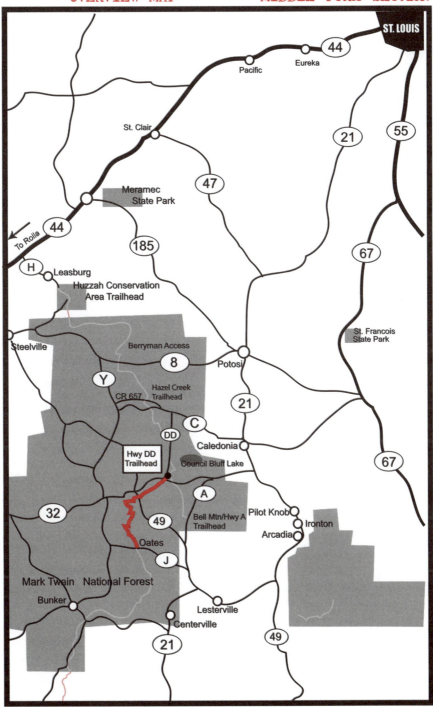

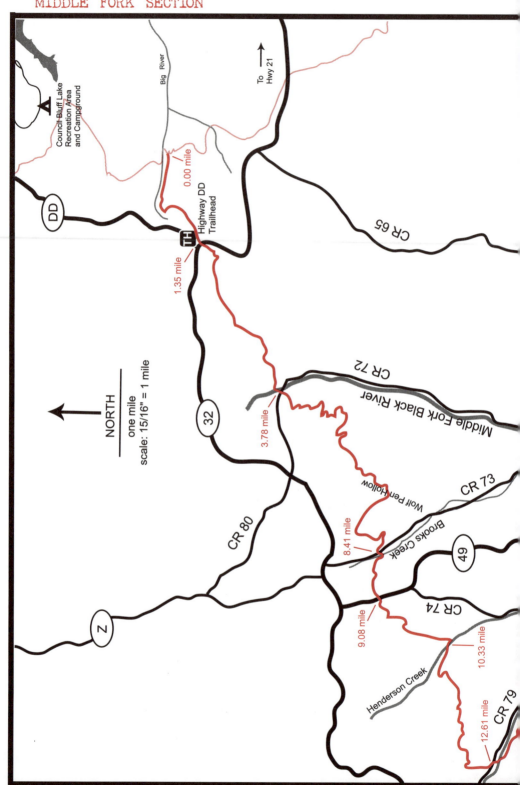

Council-Bluff Lake
Recreation Area
and Campground

Big River

To
Hwy 21

DD

0.00 mile

Highway DD
Trailhead

TH

1.35 mile

CR 65

NORTH
one mile
scale: 15/16" = 1 mile

32

CR 72

Middle Fork Black River

3.78 mile

CR 73

Wolf Pen Hollow

CR 80

8.41 mile

Brooks Creek

49

Z

9.08 mile

CR 74

10.33 mile

Henderson Creek

12.61 mile

CR 79

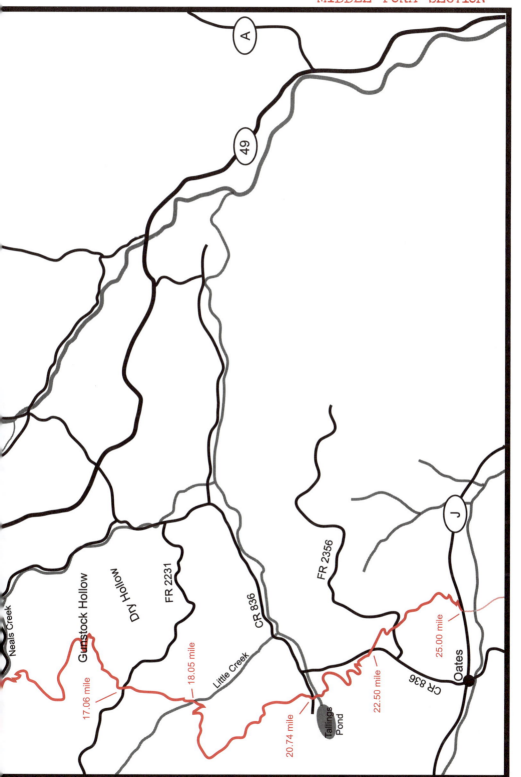

will then continue along the ridge paralleling the creek below for nearly a mile.  The trail will continue to Gunstock Hollow and then climb out of the hollow and go nearly a mile to the crossing of FR 2231.   The trail will descend about a mile to Little Creek and then climb nearly a mile to the crossing of FR 2361.

From FR 2361 the trail will travel about 1.7 miles, mostly along ridgelines and then descend to the crossing of County Road 836.  The trail will climb nearly a half-mile to the crossing of FR 2356, and travel nearly a mile along more ridgelines before descending nearly a mile to Highway J.  This will be the southern terminus of the Middle Fork Section and the northern terminus of the Karkaghne Section of the Ozark Trail.

# Trail Notes

_____

_____

_____

_____

_____

_____

_____

_____

_____

_____

_____

_____

_____

_____

_____

_____

_____

_____

_____

_____

_____

_____

_____

_____

_____

_____

_____

_____

Co-Author Peggy Welch with Mattie on the bluff overlooking the West Fork of the Black River.

# KARKAGHNE
## Section

DISTANCE 25.64 miles
TRAIL USERS foot, bike, horse

## ABOUT THIS SECTION

Pronounced "car-kag-knee" this section travels through mixed hardwood and pine forest, and meanders along Ozark hollows and ridges. Highlights along the section include Sutton Bluff on the West Fork of the Black River and Grasshopper Hollow. The bluffs are located just past the Sutton Bluff Campground and the scenic area makes a great spot to stop and have lunch. Grasshopper Hollow is North America's largest fen complex with at least fifteen fens located in the hollow. A side trip to explore the fen is well worth the trip.

Special note: From Sutton Bluff into Bee Hollow, some areas of the trail are very narrow, and are on the edge of bluffs with extreme drop-offs. It is STRONGLY SUGGESTED that mountain bikers and equestrians do not use this part of the trail. A detour route is suggested in the trail description. The Forest Service is considering a re-route due to these dangerous areas.

## HOW TO GET THERE: Trailhead Parking areas

**Highway J/ Northern Terminus-** Unmarked trailhead. There is no established parking lot here, and the turnoff for this trailhead is difficult to spot. The turn is .7 mile east of Oates (the Highway J & CR 836 intersection) and 7.6 miles west of the Highway J and Highway 49 intersection. Make a right on a little gravel road with a small OT marker. This road is rough and there isn't any really good place to park.

**Sutton Bluff Trailhead-** Highway 21 west of Lesterville and approximately 2 miles before Centerville, turn right on County Road 806. Go west approximately 7 miles and turn left at the split to County Road 849. Stay on CR 849 past Sutton Bluff Recreation Area, cross the low water bridge and continue up the hill to the Sutton Bluff Trailhead parking lot.

**Highway 72/ Highway P Trailhead Parking area-** South on Highway 21 from Centerville. Turn right (west) on Highway 72. Turn left (south) on Highway P, the trailhead parking lot is on the left side of the road.

### Trail Description North to South

The Karkaghne Section begins humbly on the south side of State Highway J, 7.6 miles west of the Highway J and Highway 49 intersection (.7 miles east of CR 836) (0 mile / 37.33.830N, 91.02.525W). It is only marked by the familiar green and white Ozark Trail markers. There isn't a convenient place to park here and the road is rough. A trailhead parking area may be constructed with the completion of the Middle Fork Section. The trail goes down the small dirt road that runs along a fence line to Brushy Creek.

Cross Brushy Creek and go about 100 yards. The trail goes to the left. To the right are some old buildings. Just after this split watch for where the trail splits again, and the OT goes to the right and

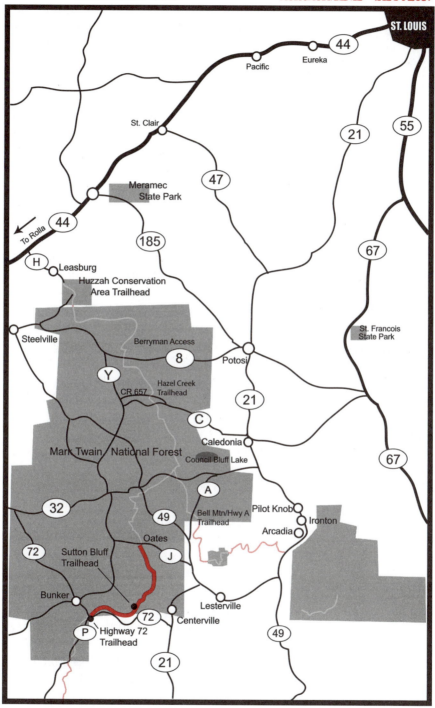

Possible Day Trips
Sutton Bluff Trailhead to
Grasshopper Hollow
(County Road 860) 10
miles (one way).

Contacts
US Forest Service-
Potosi District
Highway 8 West
Potosi, MO 63664
573-468-5427

Nature Conservancy-
2800 S. Brentwood Blvd.
St. Louis, MO 63144
314-968-1105

into the woods. Just after entering the woods, the OT veers off to the right and an ATV trail continues up the hill. A note of caution: in the next 2 miles the Ozark Trail will come to several intersections with other trails. Pay close attention at these intersections to stay on the OT. The Ozark Trail is only marked with the green and white OT trail markers through here. You will encounter several other colors of trail markers. The trail begins climbing up out of the valley, and comes to an old forest road (1.05 mile / 37.33.186N, 91.02.088W).

The OT goes straight across this old forest road and continues another mile to the crossing of another old forest road (2.03 mile / 37.32.781N, 91.01.657W). The trail goes straight across and back into the woods and soon crosses another road (2.33 mile / 37.32.632N, 91.01.412W). At the 3 mile point the trail crosses County Road 830 (37.32.162N, 91.01.311W). Special note: CR 830 is not a good road to travel, even with four-wheel drive and becomes impassible to the west of here.

The trail returns to the woods and in a short distance crosses Gunnis Creek. This is a small spring fed creek that may go dry in seasons with little rain. The trail climbs up out of the creek valley, paralleling the creek for a while then turning west, away from the creek. The trail climbs up and over the ridge to a small creek bed crossing that is usually dry (3.68 mile / 37.31.796N, 91.01.263W). The trail climbs up and over the next ridge to an old road crossing (4.29 mile /

37.31.572N, 91.01.056W). This old road comes in from the right and ends at the trail. The trail goes straight across back into the woods and climbs a little bit more before descending down this ridge and crossing another ridge. At the 4.59 mile point the trail descends through several switchback turns and comes to county road CR 828 (4.68 mile / 37.31.299N, 91.01.147W). This is a gravel road that gets some good use. The trail goes straight across and the next 1.53 miles gradually ascends through the mixed hardwood forest to the crossing of a two track (no #) gravel road (6.21 mile / 37.30.462N, 91.00.893W). The trail goes straight across and in .28 miles comes to Forest Road 2233 (6.49 mile / 37.30.280N, 91.00.766W). This is a gravel road that gets good use. Go straight across and the trail descends through the woods to the crossing of County Road 849 (7.97 mile / 37.29.693N, 91.00.223W).

This is the first crossing of CR 849. After crossing, continue downhill to County Road 806. Cross CR 806. The trail then comes to County Road 849. Turn left on 849 (a road comes in from the left, but stay on 849). Watch to the right for a vehicle pull off area. This spot offers great views from the top of the bluff of the rolling Ozark hills and the river below (WOW! spot) (9.21 mile / 37.28.721N, 91.00.211W). Continue down the hill on the road. Just before Sutton Bluff Campground the gravel road changes to pavement. The U. S. Forest Service Sutton Bluff Campground is on the left.

The Ozark Trail continues on the road and crosses the low water bridge. This "bridge" crosses the West Fork of the Black River. In very dry weather, the low water bridge may be dry, but plan on getting your feet and lower legs wet. If it has been wet and rainy, this could be impassable. If you have time available, explore the gravel bar and river bluff area. The bluffs are outstanding (WOW! spot). On the left side of the road after crossing the bridge, there is a metal guardrail that has a gap in it. The trail leaves the road here and from the gap heads uphill.

SPECIAL NOTE: It is STRONGLY suggested that mountain bikers, equestrians and hikers who do not feel comfortable with narrow bluff trails follow the gravel road (849) south 1.5 miles and turn left on to 846. Follow 846 downhill 8/10ths of a mile. There is a very rough dirt road that turns off to the left here. Follow this rough dirt road 3/10ths of a mile to meet back up with the OT. Turn right on the OT to continue on through Bee Hollow towards Grasshopper Hollow (turning left here will lead back to the dangerous area).

For those continuing from the guard rail on the narrow bluff trail, the Ozark Trail continues uphill to a shor spur trail to the trailhead parking area on County Road 849 (9.94 mile / 37.28.709N, 91.00.541W). Past the trailhead spur, the OT continues climbing along the bluffs, with great views of the West Fork of the Black River. At the 10.30 mile point is a scenic overlook with a sitting bench (37.28.475N, 91.00.581W).

The trail gets very narrow along the bluffs, use caution. Turn away from the river and the trail passes a sign that reads "Bee Fork 2.5 miles" (10.49 mile / 37.28.345N, 91.00.465W). In a short distance the trail crosses a little forest road that is not used much (10.73 mile / 37.28.246N, 91.00.422W). The trail then climbs up a hill and crosses an old forest road near the top (11.04 mile / 37.28.049W, 91.00.610W). The trail goes straight across and into a nice area with pine trees. From here the trail goes down through a low area, crosses a creek bed then climbs up and over another hill to where it gradually descends to an old forest road crossing. This is where those who use the suggested by-pass will re-join the OT (12.62 mile / 32.27.731N, 91.01.383W).

From the forest road, it is a short walk to Bee Fork. This creek should have water in it all year (12.72 mile). From the creek the trail climbs the hill on the south side of the creek. Eventually the trail levels off and follows along the hillside parallel to the creek below. Eight tenths of a mile from the Bee Fork crossing, the trail turns sharply to the left (south), and crosses a creek in less than .1 miles (at 37.27.201'N, 91.01.887'W). Keep an eye out for this crossing, as the trail seems to continue without crossing the creek. After the creek, the trail follows the hillside back to parallel above Bee Hollow. There's a nice view of the valley from here. The trail turns away from the valley, and heads uphill and further into the woods. Cross an overgrown forest road and dip down into a hollow. Pass under power lines, go to the right and the trail is on the right (14.89 mile / 37.26.950N, 91.02.426W).

After the power lines go through a narrow group of trees to the right and cross the South Branch Creek. After crossing the

Co-Author Margo Carroll at the scenic Sutton Bluff
along the Black River.

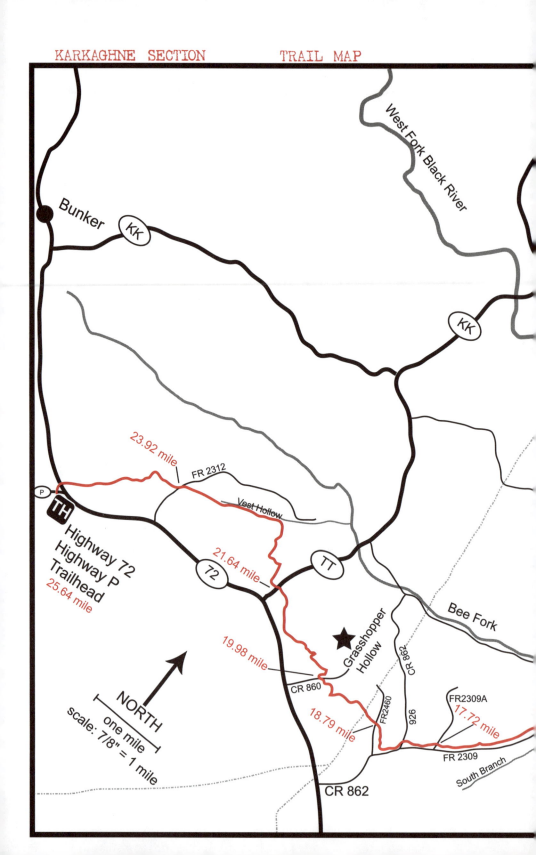

West Fork Black River

Bunker

KK

KK

23.92 mile

FR 2312

Vest Hollow

TT

21.64 mile

Highway 72
Highway P
Trailhead
25.64 mile

19.98 mile

Grasshopper
Hollow

Bee Fork

CR 862

926

FR2460

FR2309A

17.72 mile

CR 860

18.79 mile

FR 2309

South Branch

NORTH

one mile

scale: 7/8" = 1 mile

CR 862

Oates

Brushy Creek

J

CR 838

Dry Fork

Johnson Hollow

3.00 mile

CR 830

Spring

4.68 mile

Gunnis Creek

CR 826

CR 828

Missouri Branch

FR 2233

6.49 mile

West Fork Black River

Stillwell Hollow

Karkaghne Scenic Drive

7.97 mile

CR 849

Sutton Bluff
Trailhead
9.94 mile

Scenic
Views

CR 852

Horse & Bike
alternate route

CR 849

CR 806

Land Survey
Marker

15.89 mile

CR 854

TH

Sutton Bluff
Recreation Area
Campground

12.72 mile

14.93 mile

Wet Hollow

creek, the trail cuts up into the woods on the left, and begins climbing. Near the top of the climb the trail crosses an overgrown forest road (15.55 mile / 37.26.858N, 91.02.727W). The trail climbs up over a knob area with a lot of rocks, through an area that may have at one time been clear-cut, and then into a nice area with pine trees. The trail crosses another old forest road, and passes a land survey marker (15.89 mile / 37.26.589N, 91.02.784W). The trail levels and follows near the top of the ridge line and crosses two (no #) forest roads. Then cross Forest Road 2309 (17.72 mile / 37.25.468N, 91.03.992W). The next .20 mile the trail can be a bit difficult to follow, watch for markers (17.94 mile / 37.25.366N, 91.04.157W). The trail comes to State Road 926 (18.16 mile / 37.25.299N, 91.04.355W). This is a gravel road and may also be marked as County Road 862.

The trail goes straight across and in .63 miles comes to Forest Road 2460. Turn right on the road for a short distance, then turn left back onto the trail into the woods (18.79 mile / 37.25.238N, 91.04.738W). At the power lines, follow the dirt road all the way across the power cut, under all the wires, then left back into the woods to the OT (19.02 mile / 37.25.266N, 91.04.970W). Over the next mile the trail descends into Grasshopper Hollow and comes to County Road 860. To make a side trip into Grasshopper Hollow Natural Area turn right on this gravel road and follow it less than .5 miles. The area has a short nature trail that goes past an Ozark Fen and a Prairie Fen. Camping is not allowed within the Natural Area.

Continuing on the Ozark Trail from County Road 860, the trail climbs up and out of the hollow through the mixed hardwoods forest to State Highway TT (21.64 mile / 37.25.740N, 91.06.935W).

State Highway TT is a paved road and the trail goes straight across. Re-enter the woods at a spot that at times can get overgrown with briars. The trail quickly opens up to a wide path that descends to a small creek bed crossing. Climb a ridge through switchbacks to where the trail changes to single track. The trail passes an area of private property then descends, crossing several creek beds, into Vest Hollow. The hollow is close to a mile long and has several creek bed crossings and would be full of water in wet weather. The climb out of Vest Hollow is steep. Near the top, the trail crosses Forest Road 2312 (23.92 mile / 37.25.988N,

Going towards the narrow bluff segment of the
Karkaghne Section of the Ozark Trail.

91.08.681W). Over the next .9 miles, the trail goes along through a rocky area and then goes down into a bottomland forest area where it crosses several creek beds. There is a steep climb and the trail comes to a forest road (24.82 mile / 37.25.659N, 91.09.378W). Turn left on the forest road for about 20 yards and the trail cuts back into the woods on the left. The trail continues in the woods for .72 miles to the crossing of Highway 72 (25.54 miles / 37.25.182N, 91.09.937. This is a high-speed highway. Use caution crossing. The trail goes straight across and curves southeast, over towards State Road P. The Highway 72/ Highway P Trailhead is located on the east side Highway P (25.64 mile / 37.25.121N, 91.09.901W). This is the southern terminus of the Karkaghne Section and the northern terminus of the Blair Creek Section of the Ozark Trail.

# Trail Notes

John Roth overlooking the Current River.

# BLAIR CREEK
## Section

DISTANCE 25.10 miles
TRAIL USERS foot only

## ABOUT THIS SECTION

The Blair Creek Section of the Ozark Trail travels through some of the most beautiful areas of the Ozark region. Spring hikes on this section will reward the traveler with an array of blooming wildflowers including orchids and Jack-in-the Pulpits. Water is a part of the Blair Creek Section. Springs, many creeks and the Current River all add to the adventure, but remember that a fast moving creek or stream is dangerous. This is not a section to travel during or after heavy rains. Many roads in the area also become impassable due to high water. Highlights along the section include orchids, springs, caves, and some of the best river views from atop rock bluffs found anywhere on the Ozark Trail. Only foot traffic is allowed on this section.

## HOW TO GET THERE: Trailheads Parking areas
**Highway 72 Trailhead-** Located 32 miles east of Salem just south of the intersection of State Highway 72 and State Highway P. The small gravel parking area is located on the east side of State Highway P.

**Blair Fen Trailhead**- Located on County Road 235. From the Highway 72 Trailhead go 2.5 miles south on State Highway P and turn right on County Road 235. This road is marked with a sign that says Mine Road and P235. Stay on 235 for 3.18 miles and

MAPS
USGS Quadrangle maps:
Bunker, Midridge,
Powder Mill Ferry

CAMPING FACILITIES
Camping is permitted
along the trail in USFS
lands 100' from the trail.

Owls Bend Recreation
Area
Primitive campsites,
toilets, water (seasonal).

NEAREST TOWNS &
SERVICES
Bunker, Eminence.

the small gravel parking area is located on the right side set back from the road. This parking area is only signed with a small OT trail marker.

**Powder Mill Visitors Center Trailhead-** Located just off of State Highway 106, 13.2 miles east of Eminence. Watch for the sign for the Powder Mill Campground and turn right. The first right turn goes to the Visitors Center parking area. The Visitors Center is closed, but restrooms are available closeby. A short spur trail leads up to Highway 106, go straight across the highway to access the Blair Creek Section (the Current River Section begins just across the river bridge).

**Trail Description North to South**
The northern most starting point of the Blair Creek Section is located at the intersection of Highway 72 and Highway P. A small trailhead gravel parking area is located on the east side of Highway P (0.0 mile / 37.25.121N, 91.09.888W). The trail begins on the opposite side of the highway from the parking lot near the bulletin board sign. The trail travels south for 6.10 miles going past several homes and traveling on an old railroad bed to where it crosses gravel road, County Road 235 (P235) and then meets the spur trail. The spur trail is a short .16 mile walk to the Blair Fen Trailhead parking area on County Road 235. Many who travel this section of trail prefer to begin their hike from this location. From where the spur trail joins the Ozark Trail, the trail descends into the Blair Creek watershed and follows along Blair Creek.

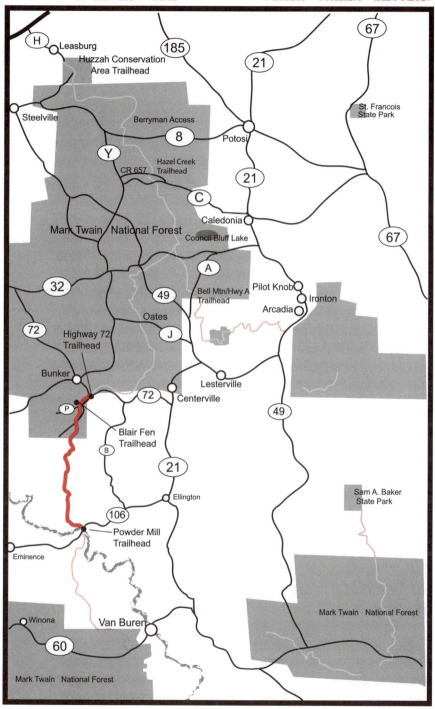

Possible Day Trips
Blair Fen Trailhead to the
Blair Creek Raised Fen 4
miles (round trip).

Contacts
US Forest Service
Salem Office
1301 South Main
Salem, MO 65560
573-729-6656

National Park Service
P.O. Box 490
Van Buren, MO 63956
573-323-4235

Missouri Department of
Conservation
P.O. Box 180
Jefferson City, MO 65102
573-468-5427

Pioneer Forest
P.O. Box 497
Salem, MO 65560
www.pioneerforest.com

MO Dept. of Natural
Resources Division of
State Parks
P.O. Box 176
Jefferson City, MO
65102-0176
www.mostateparks.com

Use caution at the 6.86 mile point and stay to the left (37.20.758N, 91.12.311W). Continue to a creek wash area and the "Y" in the trail. Go left a short distance to visit Blair Creek Raised Fen. The fen is the only raised deep muck fen in Missouri and is home to birds, turtles, crayfish and the rare marsh blue violet.

If you visit the fen be sure to come back out to the Ozark Trail the same way as you traveled down to the fen. At one time the OT was routed down through the fen, but has since been rerouted around the fen. If you should see any trail markers down by the fen do not follow them. They just lead to an overgrown mess.

From the intersection of the fen spur trail and the Ozark Trail continue on the wide trail as it travels up the hillside. Maidenhair ferns and many mosses grow on this hillside. The wide trail continues with a creek crossing (7.20 mile / 37.20.479N, 91.12.339W), and then goes through two creek wash areas to another creek crossing (7.57 mile / 37.20.285N, 91.12.187W). Just after this crossing, there is a small spring on the right that comes out of the hillside.

In seasons with little rain this spring may be dry. If hiking in the spring, watch for Jack in the Pulpit wildflowers in this area. Next the trail passes a rock outcropping that is covered with walking ferns, mosses and lichens.

At the 7.71 mile point (37.20.266N, 91.12.130W) the trail comes to the creek. Do not cross the creek here, the trail actually bends to the right, climbs up and over the hill, and becomes a small singletrack path.  Climb up and away from Blair Creek.  The trail once again becomes a wider path and comes to the gravel road crossing of P283(8.77 mile / 37.19.656N, 91.12.334W).

The Ozark Trail goes straight across gravel road P283 and  comes to a power cut area that can at times be overgrown.  The trail re-enters the woods across this power cut area, a little bit down the hill on the other side.  A registration box is located where the OT enters the Pioneer Forest (8.81 mile / 37.19.613N, 91.12.358W).  Please sign in at the registration box.  The Eastern Missouri Group of the Sierra Club maintains this section of the Ozark Trail that travels through the privately owned Pioneer Forest.  The next half mile the trail follows along a creek with many rock outcroppings and small waterfalls.  At the 9.33 mile point (37.19.331N, 91.12.682W) the trail passes the junction of the small creek with another creek and a unique rock waterfall formation.

The OT bends to the right and comes to what is referred to as "The Waterfall" WOW! Spot (9.39 mile / 37.19.339N, 91.12.721W).  The waterfall is about four or five feet tall and is a site to see after a good rainfall.  The trail ascends out of Barton Hollow on a steep path and then crosses a gravel road (9.75 mile / 37.19.276N, 91.12.994W).  Descend into Laxton Hollow.  This area is rich with wildflowers.  At the 10.81 mile point the trail meets up with a wider trail that ATV's are using and at the 10.83 mile point (37.18.590N, 91.13.177W).  The trail leaves the ATV path.  Watch closely for  trail markers here.  The trail crosses through a

"...as pretty a landscape as you'll find anywhere." –Roger Pryor
Part of the Blair Creek Section travels through the Roger Pryor Pioneer Backcountry of the Pioneer Forest.  The area is named after Roger Pryor who loved and worked to protect and encourage good forest management in the Ozarks.  The Ozark Trail within the Roger Pryor Pioneer Backcountry is managed by the Department of Natural Resources and is maintained by the Eastern Missouri Group of the Sierra Club.

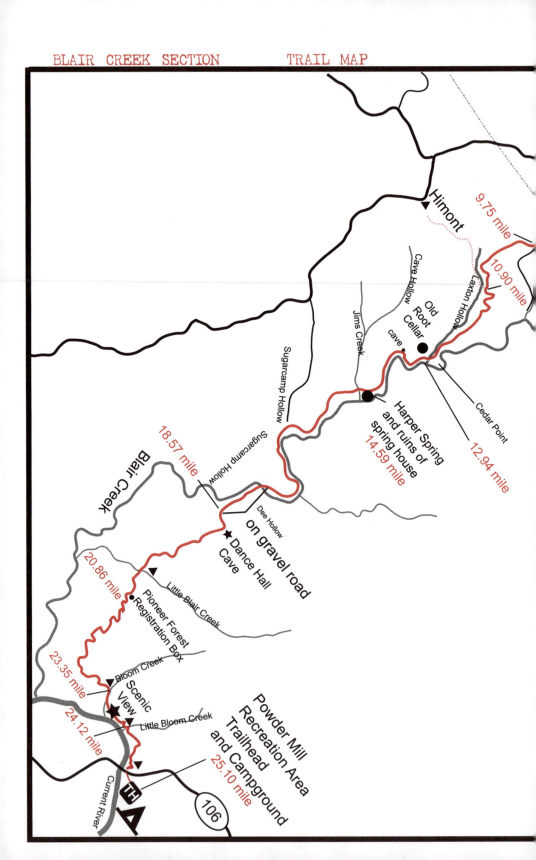

Himont

9.75 mile

10.90 mile

Cave Hollow Hollow

Old Root Cellar

Laxton Hollow

Jims Creek

cave

Cedar Point

12.94 mile

Sugarcamp Hollow

Harper Spring and ruins of spring house
14.59 mile

18.57 mile

Blair Creek

Sugarcamp Hollow

Dee Hollow

on gravel road

Dance Hall Cave

20.86 mile

Little Blair Creek

Pioneer Forest Registration Box

23.35 mile

Bloom Creek

Scenic View

24.12 mile

Little Bloom Creek

Powder Mill Recreation Area Trailhead and Campground
25.10 mile

Current River

106

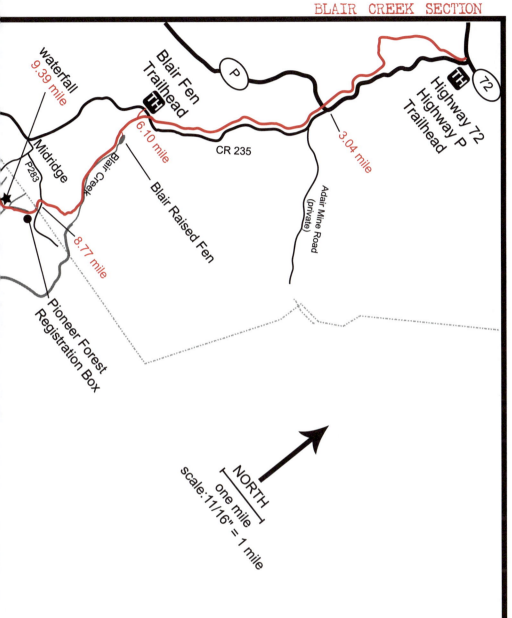

waterfall
9.39 mile

Blair Fen
Trailhead

P

6.10 mile

Midridge

P283

Blair Creek

Blair Raised Fen

CR 235

3.04 mile

Highway 72
Highway P
Trailhead

72

Adair Mine Road
(private)

8.77 mile

Pioneer Forest
Registration Box

NORTH

one mile

scale:11/16" = 1 mile

small creek then passes the intersection of the Laxton Hollow Trail. A signpost marks this intersection (10.90 mile / 37.18.598N, 91.13.123W). Over the next mile, the trail parallels Laxton Hollow and at the 11.99 mile point (37.18.058N, 91.12.627W) the trail turns right on to a double track dirt road. This old road descends through Cedar Point and down off the ridge to an intersection with a small gravel road. Turn right on the gravel road for about 5 yards and the trail turns off the gravel road to the right. The trail crosses the creek that runs through Laxton Hollow (12.90 mile / 37.17.346N, 91.12.678W). This crossing will most likely be a wet crossing. Just past the creek the trail passes an old root cellar (12.94 mile / 37.17.338N, 91.12.702W). The trail climbs up to the top of the bluff that runs along Blair Creek, running right along the edge of the bluff with a nice view of Blair Creek (WOW! Spot). Next, cross a small old overgrown dirt road and come to a small creek crossing. At this point the trail is right next to Blair Creek. Soon the trail comes to a neat rock bluff that the trail goes under (13.48 mile / 37.17.122N, 91.13.053W).

Watch on the right side for the small "Triangle Cave". Please use do not disturb any of the caves natural inhabitants. Just past the cave the trail travels up a set of natural rock steps and follows along Blair Creek for the next .7 miles to a crossing of a small old dirt road (14.18 mile / 37.16.681N, 91.12.799W). The trail goes straight across and continues through a wet seep area and then comes to a field and an old sandy road. Turn right down the road (14.28 mile / 37.16.606N, 91.12.759W). The creek flows next to this dirt road. There are blackberry bushes along the road. Just ahead on the left is the remains of the old Harper Spring house and Harpers Spring (14.59 mile / 37.16.415N, 91.12.941W). This is a neat old stone ruin. Small fish swim in the clear waters that bubble from the ground here.

In a short distance, the trail crosses Jims Creek. The trail goes from the gravel road onto a grassy old road (14.65 mile / 37.16.370N, 91.12.971W) and continues to the crossing of a dirt road (15.01 mile). The trail goes straight across. The trail comes to a crossing of a small creek area and at the 15.13 mile point use caution (37.16.035N, 91.13.112W): the trail bends to the left and then bends to the right. This spot is easy to miss. Continue up a climb, go through a small stand of pines, and into a field. Watch

82   -The Ozark Trail Guidebook

The "waterfall" along the Blair Creek Section.

for where the OT is a small trail that turns off to the left from the wider path that you are on. Pay close attention here it is easy to miss this turn (15.80 mile / 37.15.546N, 91.13.031W). Continue on the smaller path through a deep ravine. Cross a little dirt rocky road and then head out of the field and back into the forest. The trail is still following along the western side of Blair Creek and comes to a field area. A gravel road is viewable off to the left. Stay on the trail and keep your eyes open for trail markers through this area. The trail returns to the woods at the 16.81 mile point (37.15.041N, 91.12.736W). The trail makes its way down to the creek, and then travels along the creek before going up the ridge and through a black rock area.

After descending the ridge, the trail opens up into what might have been an old road. Be on the lookout, as the trail turns right off the wider path (17.21 mile / 37.15.017N, 91.12.353W). The trail follows the creek and comes out of the woods on to a gravel road. Turn right (17.37 mile / 37.14.890N, 91.12.381W) and the gravel road splits (to avoid a big muddy spot) but comes back together. Stay on the gravel road.

In about .4 mile is the crossing of Blair Creek (37.14.706N, 91.12.770W). This will be a wet crossing and after heavy rains can be impassable. After the creek, stay on the gravel road for the next .82 miles and the gravel road comes to a "Y" (18.57 mile / 37.14.168N, 91.12.886W). Go to the right. Just past the "clay waterfall" the trail turns left off the road (18.61 mile / 37.14.150N, 91.12.910W) and into a field and then into the woods. The trail climbs up through the forest and over "Dance Hall" Cave (18.87 mile / 37.14.022N, 91.12.725W). The cave is down below the ridge and has been gated shut to prevent damage to the natural habitat.

After the cave the trail crosses a well used gravel road and travels uphill .5 miles to another gravel road crossing (19.42 mile / 37.13.604N, 91.12.743W). The trail descends the next .5 miles, crosses through a creek and then goes straight across a gravel road. The wide path passes a camp spot and then crosses Little Blair Creek. Next the trail crosses an old grassy road (20.39 mile / 37.12.862N, 91.12.934W). The trail begins a steep climb for the next .48 miles and then crosses a gravel road (20.86 mile / 37.12.500N, 91.12.809W).

Missouri Primrose in bloom.

On an afternoon hike.

The OT leaves the Pioneer Forest here. The trail descends, and the single track path joins an old road. The trail travels on the old road into a glade area. Watch closely for where the trail cuts to the left and back into the woods (21.17 mile / 37.12.333N, 91.12.613W). The trail leaves the glade area next to a large cedar tree. This area can be tough to follow the trail through. In a short distance the trail goes straight down through a rough rocky area and then makes a right turn (21.33 mile / 37.12.200N, 91.12.563W). The trail gets a bit overgrown with small trees and then runs along a rock ledge. It crosses up and over the ledge and bends and begins descending into Pogue Hollow. Once in the hollow, the trail crosses a small creek (21.65 mile / 37.12.009N, 91.12.514W). The next 1.5 miles the trail travels through the mixed hardwood forest and passes a small spring that is on the left (23.20 mile / 37.11.575N, 91.11.867W). The trail joins up with a narrow grassy road. This is a good place to camp (37.11.572N, 91.11.837W). The OT continues down the grassy path to the right through a rocky creek bed and to the crossing at Blooms Creek (23.35 mile / 37.11.488N, 91.11.745W).

After the creek crossing, watch closely for where the OT cuts off to the left. This can be an easy turn to miss (23.48 mile / 37.11.422N, 91.11.665W). The trail begins to climb and at the 23.69 mile point the trail comes to a "T". If you go to the right a short distance you will get your first views of the Current River through the trees.

At the "T" intersection the OT continues to the left and soon comes to a great bluff top view of the Current River WOW! spot (23.87 mile / 37.11.405N, 91.11.369W). This spot just might be the best place on the Ozark Trail for outstanding river views. Missouri Primrose wildflowers bloom in this clearing during late April. Not far from here there is a good flat spot to camp that gets used frequently (37.11.417N, 91.11.354W).

The trail descends through several switchback turns, crosses Little Bloom Creek (24.12 mile / 37.11.502N, 91.11.204W), and then climbs back up along the bluffs. The next .5 miles the trail travels along the ridge above the Current River. In spots the trail gets very narrow before it comes to another scenic area with a great view (24.84 mile / 37.11.288N, 91.10.749W).

The Highway 106 bridge over the Current River is visible at this overlook . The trail continues .25 miles to Highway 106. The Current River Section of the Ozark Trail begins across the highway bridge. This bridge gets high-speed traffic use, so stay well to the side when crossing. If you have parked at the old visitors center parking lot the spur trail to the lot is located across Highway 106 on the east side of the bridge. This is the southern terminus of the Blair Creek Section of the Ozark Trail.

Yellow Lady Slipper Orchid.

# Trail Notes

Klepzig Mill on Rocky Creek.

# CURRENT RIVER
## Section

DISTANCE 30.00 miles
TRAIL USERS foot traffic only

## ABOUT THIS SECTION

This is an exceptionally beautiful section of the Ozark Trail. The trail traverses through the Current River watershed, passing through Peck Ranch Conservation Area, which is rich with turkey, deer and other wildlife. Indian Creek and Rocky Creek are scenic with boulder filled creek beds, shut-ins, waterfalls and pools that offer the trail traveler many wonderful scenic pleasures. A short side trip to the forty-foot tall Rocky Falls is worth the hike. The climb up Stegall Mountain is both challenging and rewarding with beautiful panoramic views. Highlights: The Current River, Shut-Ins, Indian Creek, Rocky Creek, Klepzig Mill, Stegall Mountain, Peck Ranch, Mint Spring, side trip to Rocky Falls.

## HOW TO GET THERE: Trailhead Parking areas

**Powder Mill Visitors Center Trailhead-** The northern terminus trailhead is located 13.2 miles east of Eminence, just off State Highway 106. Watch for the sign for the Powder Mill Campground and turn right. The first right turn goes to the Visitors Center parking area. The Visitors Center is closed, but restrooms are available closeby. A short spur trail leads up to Highway 106. The Current River Section begins just across the river bridge.

MAPS
USGS Quadrangle maps:
Powder Mill Ferry, Stegall
Mtn, Fremont, Van Buren
South

CAMPING FACILITIES
NO CAMPING along trail
in MDC Peck Ranch.

Camping is permitted
along the trail in USFS
lands 100' from the trail.

Owls Bend Recreation
Area
Primitive campsites,
toilets, water (seasonal).

Peck Ranch
Conservation Area
Campground
Primitive in designated
areas only, restrooms and
water (seasonal)

NEAREST TOWNS &
SERVICES
Eminence, Van Buren,
Winona.

**Powder Mill Ferry (2 mile) Trailhead-** Located two miles south west from the Powder Mill Visitors Center Trailhead. To get there go 11 miles on Highway 106 west from Eminence and turn right on the unmarked road that leads to where the Powder Mill Ferry use to run(1.6 miles west of the Current River Bridge). Go to the end of this road and turn right on an unmarked road that goes downhill and changes to gravel. Follow this road 1.15 miles to the Trailhead located in a field on the right.

**Rocky Falls Access-** Located at the National Park Services Rocky Falls parking area. Restrooms and water are available here (seasonal). A spur trail accesses the Ozark Trail. From Highway 106 take Highway H south 3.86 miles and turn left on Highway NN. Go two miles and turn right on County Road 526 and Rocky Falls is just a little over a half mile.

**Peck Ranch Trailhead-** Located 3 miles east of Highway H on County Road 514. The parking area is located on the left.

**Highway 60 Trailhead-** Located 3.9 miles west of Van Buren on Highway 60. The trailhead is located on the south side of the highway and is large enough to turn a horse trailer around.

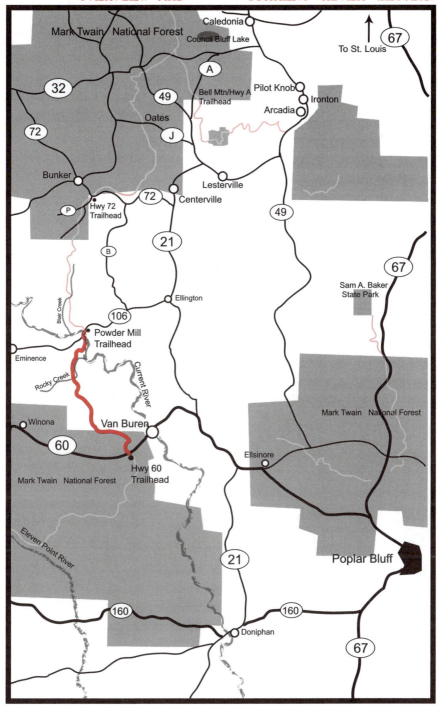

CURRENT RIVER SECTION
## Trail Description North to South
The Current River Section begins on the south side of Highway 106, just west of the Current River Bridge. There is no parking area here, but parking is available at the Powder Mill Visitors center and a spur trail connects to State Highway 106. It is just a short hike over the Current River bridge to a sign along the south side of the highway that marks the beginning of the Current River section of the Ozark Trail.

The trail goes up the small hill and through some cedar trees. Near the half mile point the trail descends to a paved road (.60 mile / 37.10.834N, 91.10.607W). Go straight across the paved road and continue down the hill on the paved road. The road bends to the left and changes to gravel, and takes you to the registration box (.72 mile / 37.10.828N, 91.10.545W).

The registration box is located on the right side of the road. Across the road the trail re-enters the woods. This part of the trail is relatively flat traveling along the Current River. The trail comes to a wooden bridge and then goes back out to the gravel road (.90 mile). Go left here on the road for about 5 yards and the trail re-enters the woods on the left side. The trail travels through this relatively level grassy area for the next 1.07 miles, crossing two more wooden bridges and then coming to a sandy dirt road (1.97 mile / 37.09.899N, 91.10.008W). Turn right on this road and continue .16 miles to a grassy Ozark Trail parking area (2.13 mile / 37.09.819N, 91.10.138W). Over the next 1.25 miles the trail follows along the western side of the Current River, and climbs several ridges that have some great areas that over look the river.

Cross Little Indian Creek (3.38 mile / 37.08.904N, 91.10.548W). Go .5 miles to Indian Creek. The trail runs along Indian Creek for 1.95 miles with several more crossings as it makes it's way around Barnett Mountain. Indian Creek is a great place to view small rock shelves, shut-ins and small waterfalls. The trail turns away from Indian Creek and becomes rockier as it goes uphill and runs along the right side of a little creek bed (5.33 mile / 37.08.250N, 91.11.783W). This is a good climb up and over the ridge to where the trail descends down to the valley and Rocky Creek.

The trail crosses Rocky Creek at the Klepzig Mill and shut-ins area (WOW! spot). This is an exceptionally beautiful area.

Possible Day Hikes

Rocky Falls to Peck Ranch 4.86 miles (one way).

Powder Mill Ferry (2 mile) Trailhead to Peck Ranch 11.09 miles (one way).

Contacts
US Forest Service
Eleven Point Office
Highway 19
Winona, MO 65588
573-325-4233

National Park Service
P.O. Box 490
Van Buren, MO 63956
573-323-4235

Missouri Department of Conservation
P.O. Box 180
Jefferson City, MO 65102
573-468-5427

The Walter Klepzig Mill and Farm is part of the Ozark National Scenic Riverway and is on the National Register of Historic Places. The mill was built in 1912, the National Park Service discourages visitors from entering the structure because it is dangerous. Cross the well-used dirt road, and the trail follows the two track path through the grassy valley area. The trail returns to the side of Rocky Creek (WOW! spot) as the OT goes between Mill Mountain and Buzzard Mountain. Watch closely as the trail goes uphill towards Highway NN for where the trail turns right on to the single-track trail (7.52 mile / 37.06.837N, 91.11.945W).

At paved Highway NN (7.93 mile / 37.03.585N, 91.12.106W) turn right and follow the highway. Just after crossing Rocky Creek watch for the OT on the left side. There is a small area here that has been used to park vehicles but it is not a real parking lot. Continue south and cross through Denning Hollow. The trail then climbs up and over a hill. As the trail flattens out near the valley there is an area that can get overgrown a bit. At the 8.83 mile point the trail crosses Rocky Creek again (37.05.763N, 91.12.106W). Just past this point the trail comes to an intersection with a small two track grassy road. To get to Rocky Falls, turn right here and follow this spur trail .45 miles to the falls. This detour is well worth the trip. Rocky Falls is a forty-foot tall waterfall, and the huge rock formations dwarf the surrounding scenery. This is a developed NPS day use area with picnic tables and pit toilets.

Upon returning to the OT, continue gradually climbing and crossing some creek beds through Kelley Hollow. The trail crosses a foot bridge (9.79 mile / 37.05.105N, 91.11.562W) and continues uphill. This is the beginning of the 1.55 mile climb up Stegall Mountain. Continue up through several switchbacks, and the trail crosses an old road that doesn't show on the USGS maps (10.20 mile / 37.04.854N, 91.11.298W). This area shows signs of a past fire. The summit of Stegall Mountain (11.34 mile / 37.04.289N, 91.11.302W) is a beautiful glade area, dotted with exposed granite (WOW! Spot). The views are outstanding and rival those along the Taum Sauk Section. The trail along the top of the mountain is thinly marked with the green and white OT trail markers and rock cairns, so keep your eyes open and travel with care and caution through the glade areas. The descent from the top of Stegall Mountain is rough and steep through boulder fields and stands of pine trees.

The trail levels out and at the 12.16 mile point crosses a dirt road (37.03.929N, 91.11.636W). At the 13.05 mile point (37.03.673N, 91.10.978W) the trail comes to a dirt road in a stand of pine trees. Turn right and follow the road .12 miles to where the trail turns left off the dirt road (13.17 mile). Note: The Peck Ranch Trailhead and parking area can be accessed by continuing .4 miles on the dirt road.(37.03.185N, 91.11.055W).

Continue on the OT on the small trail that climbs up and over to a dirt forest road crossing (14.30 mile / 37.03.269N, 91.10.436W). The trail parallels the road for the next .47 miles and at times can get over grown. At the 14.77-mile point the trail turns away from the road in a more southerly direction down towards Mule Hollow. Cross another forest road (14.90 mile / 37.03.004N, 91.10.058W). The trail looks like it might curve to the right but it doesn't. Cross another forest road (14.92 mile / 37.20.981N, 91.10.052W). After crossing the road, there is a wildlife pond to the right, off the trail. Descend a hill and a small low rock wall comes into view. The trail cuts off to the right prior to the low rock wall. Use caution here; at times the trail marker is missing that marks this turn (15.08 mile / 37.02.945N, 91.09.951W).

For .2 mile the OT is down in Mule Hollow and follows a small creek bed. As the hollow widens at the far end the trail leaves the hollow to the left. The next .80 miles the trail climbs up and

Rocky Point Glade, in the
Peck Ranch Conservation Area.

across a hill to a point where the road below is visible. This is also the beginning of the beautiful Rocky Point Glade (WOW! Spot) (16.14 mile / 37.02.665N, 91.09.783W). The trail descends steeply through the glade to a gravel road.

Cross the road in the valley (16.29 mile / 37.02.367N, 91.09.297W). The trail continues into the lowland woods. In the next .36 miles the trail has some areas that get overgrown. Be alert for trail markers. Cross through Mill Creek, which is dry a lot of the year. The trail re-enters the woods down to the right side and continues through some areas with spotty overgrown sections. Climb up to a dirt road crossing (16.65 mile / 37.02.220N, 91.09.264W).

The trail goes straight across, then downhill and crosses a creek bed. Just after the creek the trail comes to a grassy road (16.74 mile, 37.02.154N, 91.09.198W). Turn right and proceed on the grassy road to the wildlife pond (16.93 mile, 37.02.004N, 91.09.261W). In the spring this area is loud with the sounds of frogs. The trail crosses over the dam of this pond, and then parallels the pond. This area can get very overgrown. Be alert for trail markers. The next .50 miles the trail runs down in Pritchard Hollow and along the rocky creek bed, crossing it several times. At the 17.41 mile point the trail comes to a place that can be confusing. The trail goes across the gravel wash area and continues on the wider old road path (37.01.635N, 91.09.420W).

At the "Y" in the trail go to the left and continue on the wider old road path (17.47 mile). Keep alert for where the trail turns off this road to the left (17.52 mile / 37.01.567N, 91.09.467W) on to the smaller trail. The trail climbs and crosses a gravel road (17.87 mile, 37.01.297N, 91.09.511W). The trail goes straight across and gets rockier. Some parts are moss lined and in springtime several Birds Foot Violets will be in bloom in this area. After cresting the top of this climb the trail descends through an area that has burned then passes a wildlife pond on the right (18.45 mile , 37.00.920N, 91.09.442W). We encountered only two snakes when we hiked the entire Ozark Trail; it was here that we met our most startling. Just as we began to step over a fallen tree trunk the "rattling" began. Fortunately for us, it was only a Speckled King snake beating its tail against the ground making the sound of a rattle. Speckled King snakes are nonvenomus and are very good for the environment. The snake didn't strike and just made its way away from us. We did the same, feeling fortunate that we had the opportunity to see the beautiful snake and fortunate that none of us (including the snake) were harmed. All snakes in Missouri are protected by law, please do not harm or disturb any snakes that you may encounter.

In less than a tenth of a mile the trail comes to a section that gets overgrown with briars (18.54 mile / 37.00.860N, 91.09.373W). The next .57 miles the trail parallels a gravel road just inside the tree line and comes to a crossing of a gravel road (19.11 mile / 37.00.517N, 91.09.134W). This gravel road is the perimeter road of Peck Ranch Conservation Area. Straight across the road the trail exits Peck Ranch through the fence. The trail goes through the food plot planting towards the right entering the woods onto the singletrack trail.

In Midco Hollow the trail can get a little overgrown and can be a little "thin", so keep your eyes open for trail markers. Through the hollow the trail is relatively flat and follows and crosses a creek wash. The trail comes to a clearing (19.91 mile, 36.59.945N, 91.08.755W). Go to the right, head into the stand of pine trees and watch for markers. In a short distance, the trail passes a US Forest Service Boundary sign (19.95 mile, 36.59.901N, 91.08.740W). Continue through the Midco Hollow bottoms to the dirt, gravel road (20.30 mile / 36.59.708N, 91.08.468W). Go straight across then up hill. The next mile of trail climbs up and along a ridge through a forest area that has burned. Little new growth and fallen dead trees can make this area tough to navigate. Stay alert for trail markers.

At the top of the ridge the trail bends to the left and comes to a clearing. A camp area is located to the right. The trail re-enters the woods just past the camp spot and across the dirt road (21.46 mile / 36.59.659N, 91.07.460W. The trail goes downhill for the next .4 miles past some neat areas with big rocks covered in lichens. The trail makes another climb then descends steeply. At the bottom there is a grassy road (22.96 mile / 36.59.633N, 91.06.242W). Turn left onto the grassy road. Follow this grassy road .27 miles and stay alert. The trail will turn off this road to the right on a small trail (23.23 mile / 36.59.670N, 91.06.193W).

The trail crosses a small creek bed then heads uphill. Go

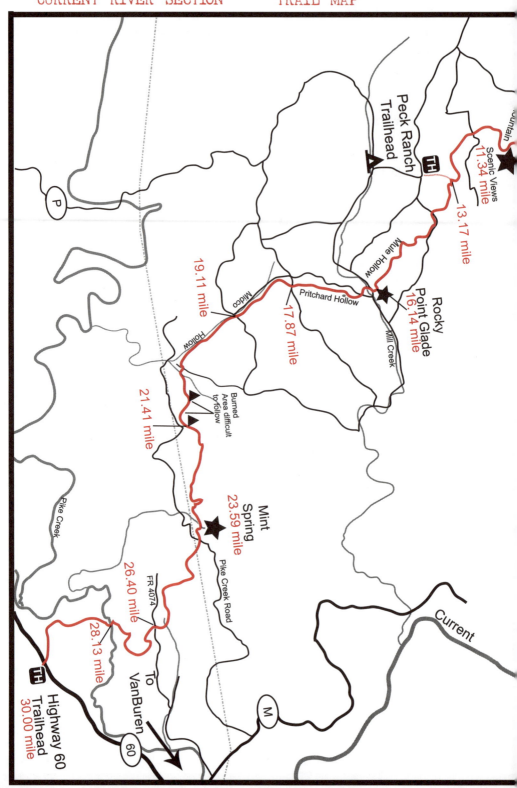

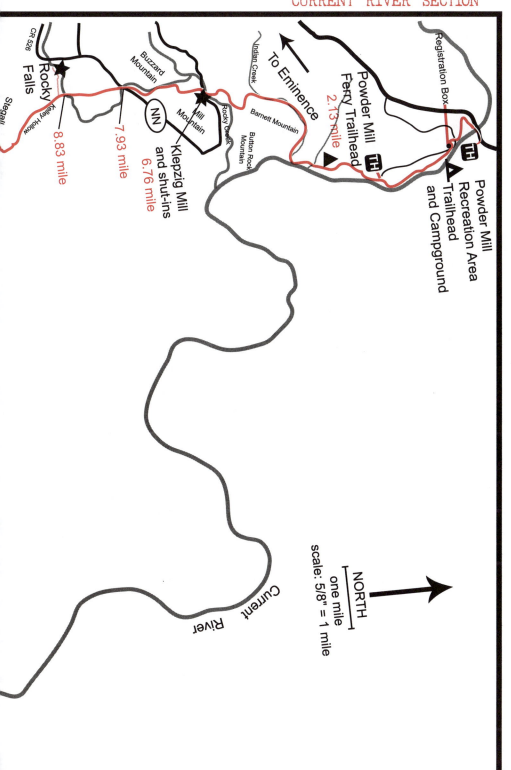

Registration Box

Powder Mill
Ferry Trailhead
2.13 mile

To Eminence

Indian Creek

Barnett Mountain

Button Rock
Mountain

Rocky Creek

Powder Mill
Recreation Area
Trailhead
and Campground

Buzzard
Mountain

Mill
Mountain

NN

Klepzig Mill
and shut-ins
6.76 mile

CR 526

Rocky
Falls

Stegall

Kelley Hollow

8.83 mile

7.93 mile

Current
River

NORTH
one mile
scale: 5/8" = 1 mile

Mint Spring

another .36 miles through the forest to Mint Spring (WOW! spot)(23.59 mile / 36.59.700N, 91.05.909W). The spring comes out of a rocky opening on the hillside on the left. This spring is usually a good source for water, but has been known to go dry during times with little rain. Be sure to purify the water and use care to preserve this wonderful spot.

The trail climbs up out of the little spring valley and continues .44 miles to a gravel road (24.03 mile / 36.59.687N, 91.05.594W). Cross the gravel road and the trail goes downhill, through a power cut (24.19 mile / 36.59.626N, 91.05.448W), back into the woods and down the hill. At the bottom the trail levels out and crosses a small creek (24.34 mile / 36.59.553N, 91.05.325W). The trail comes to FR 4074 (24.89 mile / 36.59.458N, 91.05.254W). FR 4074 is not a drivable road at this junction. The trail goes straight across and climbs up and over a ridge and crosses FR 4074 again (26.40 mile / 36.58.983N, 91.04.292W). Cross the road (which is drivable here) and the trail travels along the top edge of the ridgeline. Go down the opposite side through some pines. Cross a small creek bed, then follow the trail along the creek bed.

Stay alert here for a HARD RIGHT TURN (27.46 mile / 36.58.560N, 91.03.946W). The trail appears to go straight ahead towards a No Trespassing sign, but then cuts off to the right. Go up hill through some pine trees on a rocky knob. This is a very pretty spot. The trail leaves the knob heading downhill. At the 27.75 mile point the trail crosses a small creek (36.58.603N, 91.04.192W). After the creek follow the trail to the left, then watch for where it turns off to the right (27.84 mile / 36.58.524N, 91.04.239W).

The trail turns south, and goes over a wooden step up barrier, crosses the road, then goes up and over the next step up barrier (28.13 mile / 36.58.426N, 91.04.445W). The trail turns left and travels about 50 yards along the fence to where it crosses Pike Creek. This is a big creek, and will be a wet crossing. Once across the creek, the OT goes to the right over another step up barrier. Follow the wide path along the fence and up the hill through another step up barrier. After this barrier, the trail is no longer fenced in. Go .68 miles and the trail comes to an old forest road, CR 111 (29.10 mile / 36.57.724N, 91.04.524W). Cross the road and you will soon pass signs marking private property on the right of the trail.

In .25 miles, the trail comes to a registration box (29.73 mile / 36.57.488N, 91.04.104W). It's just .21 miles to Highway 60 from the registration box. Highway 60 is a paved major roadway. Use extra caution when crossing. On the southern side of the highway is the Highway 60 Ozark Trail Trailhead parking area (30.00 mile / 36.57.401N, 91.03.912W). This is a large gravel parking lot. This is the southern terminus of the Current River Section of the Ozark Trail.

# Trail Notes

Between the Rivers and amidst the trees.

# BETWEEN THE RIVERS
## Section

27.50 miles
TRAIL USERS foot, bike, horse

### About this section

This section is appropriately named Between the Rivers as it lies between the Current River and the Eleven Point River Sections of the Ozark Trail. Water can be scarce along this section during most of the year. The northern trailhead is located off Highway 60 near Van Buren. From there the trail travels south through Wildhorse Hollow and the Devils Run drainage. Shannon County is home to some of the last remaining wild horses in Missouri. This section travels through extensive forestlands with abundant oak and hickory trees.

### HOW TO GET THERE: Trailhead Parking areas

**Highway 60 Trailhead-** Located 3.9 miles west of Van Buren on Highway 60. The trailhead is located on the south side of the highway and is large enough to turn a horse trailer around.

**Sinking Creek Lookout Tower Trailhead-** Located on Forest Road 3152. From Highway 60 take Highway J south 8.75 miles, turn right on Forest Road 3152 and the trailhead is located .92 miles on the left side.

MAPS
USGS Quadrangle maps:
Van Buren South, Handy,
Wilderness, Greer

CAMPING FACILITIES
Camping is permitted
along the trail in USFS
lands 100' from the trail.

NEAREST TOWNS &
SERVICES
The city of Van Buren is
located 3.9 miles west of
the northern trailhead.
Motels, groceries, gas.

The city of Alton is
located 17 miles
southwest of the Forest
Road 3152 Trailhead.

**Forest Road 3152 Trailhead-** Located on Forest Road 3152, 5 miles southwest of the Sinking Creek Lookout Tower Trailhead and is large enough to turn a horse trailer around.

## Trail Description North to South

Begin at the Highway 60 Trailhead located 3.9 miles west of Van Buren on Highway 60. The trailhead is located on the south side of the highway and is large enough to turn a horse trailer around in. Note: The USGS Van Buren South Quadrangle map shows the OT following a road from this parking area, that is incorrect. From this parking area you access the OT by taking the very short spur trail located on the eastern side of the parking lot. At the trail junction turn right (south). The trail parallels the road for .39 miles, past a few houses. I encountered a large dog here who a bit frightening, but it did not attack. He gave us a scare. The trail comes to the registration box (.39 miles / 36.57.118N, 91.03.823W). In the next half mile the trail climbs up and over a ridge and then passes a Carter County land survey marker (.85 mile / 36.56.926N, 91.03.583W). The trail is mostly level here, then crosses an old road that doesn't show on the USGS map (.87 mile / 36.56.929N, 91.03.567W). In the next .40 miles the trail gains elevation, getting steeper the closer it gets to the road (1.51 mile / 36.56.805N, 91.02.964W). At the road crossing the trail heads downhill into Wildhorse Hollow.

Caledonia

Mark Twain National Forest

Council Bluff Lake

Salem

(A)

(32)

(49)

Bell Mtn/Hwy A
Trailhead

Pilot Knob
Ironton
Arcadia

(72)

Oates

(19)

(J)

Bunker

Lesterville

(P)

Hwy 72
Trailhead

(72)

Centerville

(49)

(B)

(21)

Blair Creek

Ellington

(106)

Powder Mill
Trailhead

Eminence

Current River

Rocky Creek

Winona

Van Buren

(60)

Fremont

Hwy 60
Trailhead

Ellsinore

(19)

(J)

Eleven Point River

FR 3152

FR 3152
Trailhead

Mark Twain  National Forest

(21)

To Poplar
Bluff

Alton

(160)

Doniphan

(160)

(142)

Possible Day Trips
Sinking Creek Lookout
Tower Trailhead to the
Forest Road 3152
Trailhead 6.9 miles
(one-way)

Contacts
US Forest Service
Eleven Point Office
Highway 19
Winona, MO 65588
573-325-4233

The trail stays in Wildhorse Hollow for .86 miles, and passes an old rusty car, which is a well-known landmark (2.46 mile / 36.56.224N, 91.02.776W). A little ways down the hollow the trail makes a bend to the left where it begins a steep climb (2.73 mile / 36.56.012N, 91.02.724W). At a wildlife pond, the OT continues straight ahead to where a forest road goes to the right. (3.16 mile / 36.55.900N, 91.02.289W). If you are ever out on this section of trail on a frosty morning, watch for frost flowers. On a January hike there were many here. The trail comes to a nice pine tree area (3.53 mile / 36.55.640N, 91.02.126W), and then crosses an old forest road (3.62 mile / 36.55.546N, 91.02.159W). After a little bit of a climb, cross Forest Road 3255 (3.82 mile / 36.55.415N, 91.02.269W). The trail skirts the eastern edge of a farm and then goes around the southeastern corner. Pass a small pond into more pine trees. Begin downhill and cross a creek bed that gets a lot of run off water. Just past the creek bed the OT turns left (4.45 mile / 36.55.069N, 91.02.745W). The trail descends to another creek bed crossing then begins to climb and joins an old forest road. Near the top of this climb the OT turns to the left off of the old road (5.03 mile / 36.54.659N, 91.02.867W). The trail descends to a creek bed crossing then back up and over a hill to Chilton Creek, which is not a reliable water source (5.56 mile / 36.54.297N, 91.03.152W). The trail continues uphill and comes to County Road 210 (5.90 mile / 36.54.066N, 91.03.291W).

There is no parking area at County road 210, but there's evidence that some people have pulled off the side of the road here. Cross this dirt road. The trail continues and begins downhill, and comes to the crossing of State Highway C (6.23 mile / 36.54.066N, 91.03.291W). There is no parking area here, but it looks like some have just pulled off the road onto the grass here. Cross the paved road and continue downhill. Towards the bottom cross a creek bed, climb a small hill, and descend to another creek bed. It is a gradual uphill to Forest Road 3254L. Crest the climb and descend. You'll notice the trail gets rockier as you enter Devils Run (WOW! Spot) (7.12 mile / 36.53.355N, 91.04.169W).

Years and years of water rushing down through the "Run" has created quite a neat area, filled with boulders and a creek bed that will fill to dangerously high levels after a rain. Here the trail travels on an old railroad bed. There are remnants of the old railroad bed that once ran through here.

Continue downhill along the side of Devils Run, then cross through Devils Run (7.59 mile / 36.52.983N, 91.04.118W). This is a 6-8 foot ravine, do not attempt to cross in high water. The trail ascends out of the "Run" and traverses up to where the trail crosses Forest Road 3253A (8.05 mile / 36.52.658N, 91.04.281W). Cross the road and the trail continues in the forest for just about a mile to the crossing of Forest Road 3253 (9.04 mile / 36.52.037N, 91.03.990W). The trail goes straight across and becomes wider like an old road. The trail changes back to single track as it climbs a hill. In a short distance the trail becomes wide again. Down in Hog Hollow cross a small creek 9.80 mile / 36.51.850N, 91.04.590W).

In Hog Hollow the trail comes to a crossing of a two-track dirt road (9.88 mile / 36.51.860N, 91.04.670W). Through this area the trail is really pretty with many ferns, mosses and lichens. Proceed the next .38 miles of ascent out of Hog Hollow and at the top begin back down through switchbacks (10.60 mile / 36.51.604N, 91.05.224W). Pass the Bristol Cemetery and the trail crosses Forest Road 4006. This gravel road is in good condition. The trail remains fairly level to where it crosses Big Barren Creek (10.98 mile / 36.51.363N, 91.05.167W). This creek can be nearly dried up or a very wide rush of water. For the next .15 miles the trail remains fairly level, then it makes a good climb up. Continue along

A trailside frost flower.

this ridge for .50 miles. Then the trail descends .20 miles and comes to County Road 167 (12.10 mile / 36.50.744N, 91.05.186W). Cross CR167 and begin the gradual climb to where the trail passes through a power cut (12.73 mile / 36.50.347N, 91.05.550W). Continue .18 miles to a small dirt road (12.91 mile / 36.50.347N, 91.05.732W). Cross the road and follow along the top of the ridge for .39 miles.

Descend into Spring Hollow (13.50 mile / 36.50.326N, 91.06.225W) and cross the creek bed that is usually dry. Then cross gravel road FR 4002, then head back uphill. The OT continues through the oak, hickory and scattered pine forest to the top of the hill then descends, crossing a small creek and passing a land survey marker (14.37 mile / 36.50.274N, 91.06.646W). Continue on, as the trail levels, pass an area that can get overgrown and now down in Still House Hollow. Cross the creek (14.57 mile / 36.50.413N, 91.06.789W) that has water in it most of the year. The trail climbs the next .53 miles to Forest Road 4822 (15.01 mile / 36.50.392N, 91.07.189W). The trail continues the next .50-mile to where it descends down to a crossing of an old overgrown dirt road (15.86 mile / 36.50.308N, 91.07.930W). Go a short distance to a creek crossing and to where the OT joins up with an ATV/jeep trail for about 50 yards. Then the ATV/jeep trail goes up the hill and the OT goes back into the woods (15.97 mile / 36.50.351N, 91.08.027W). There is a nice view of the North Prong Cedar Bluff Creek just below on the right. Cross a creek bed and along the left is a neat rock wall (16.19 mile / 36.50.335N, 91.08.244W).

The trail crosses the North Prong Cedar Bluff Creek again and climbs up to a "T" intersection (17.37 mile / 36.50.561N, 91.09.398W). The forest road goes off to the right and the OT goes to the left. In a short distance, the forest road curves off to the left away from OT, and the OT goes straight across the rocky North Prong Creek (17.51 mile / 36.50.460N, 91.09.461W). The next 1-mile the trail follows the North Prong Cedar Bluff Creek bed and gradually ascends to State Highway J (19.45 mile / 36.50.516N, 91.11.093W). Cross the highway and descend .30 mile to Cotham Pond (19.75 mile / 36.50.595N, 91.11.447W). At the pond there is a place to camp. Go to the right around the lake, cross the road (FR 4033) and continue across the dam. The dam can get overgrown with brush and briars. The next .50 miles the trail

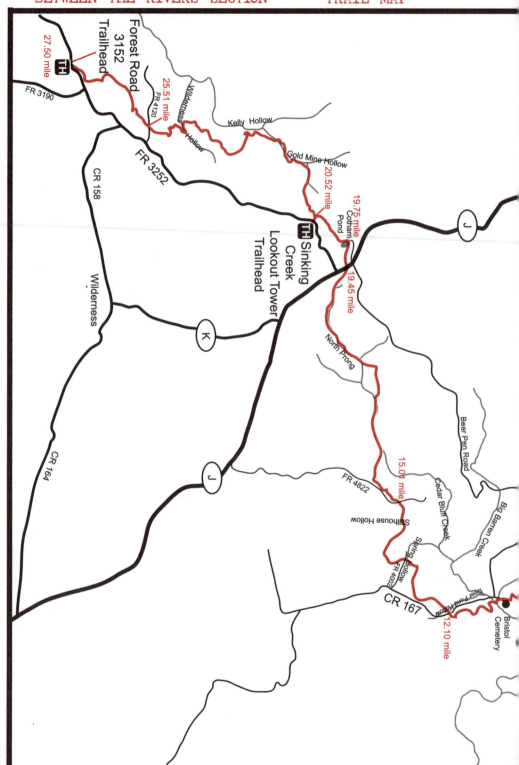

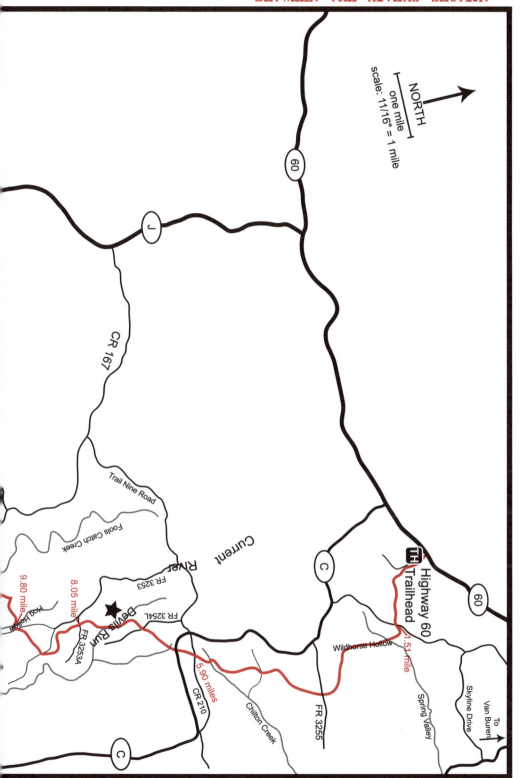

NORTH

one mile
scale: 11/16" = 1 mile

60

J

CR 167

Trail Nine Road

Fools Catch Creek

Current

River

FR 3253

FR 3254L

Devils Run

FR 3253A

Hog Hollow

9.80 mile

8.05 mile

C

C

Highway 60
Trailhead

Wildhorse Hollow

FR 3255

Spring Valley

Skyline Drive

To
Van Buren

1.51 mile

5.90 miles

CR 210

Chilton Creek

60

The old car in Wildhorse Hollow.

gradually climbs to a power cut (20.37 mile / 36.50.385N, 91.11.938W). Continue .15 miles to the spur trail that goes to the Sinking Creek Lookout Tower Trailhead parking area.

The trailhead is just .10 from here. Continue on the OT and the trail comes to a forest road, but does not join the forest road here. The OT makes a curving right hand turn away from the road (20.75 mile / 36.50.227N, 91.12.173W). This turn is easy to miss! The trail descends towards Goldmine Hollow, crosses several creek beds, then follows along above the creek (21.83 mile / 36.50.208N, 91.13.005W) to the crossing of the creek bed in the heart of the hollow (22.18 mile / 36.50.081N, 91.13.210W). Cross an old forest road (22.43 mile / 36.50.018N, 91.13.437W) and pass through more rocky wash areas. The trail climbs up to an old forest road crossing (23.53 mile / 36.49.354N, 91.13.403W). The trail follows along this ridge for nearly a mile then descends down into Wilderness Hollow. Cross the creek bed. Go .17 miles and cross an old forest road (24.88 mile / 36.48.756N, 91.14.077W). From here the trail climbs to near the top of the ridge and crosses Forest Road 4120 (25.51 mile / 36.48.409N, 91.14.147W). The trail goes straight across and follows along a ridgeline before descending into Fox Hollow. In the hollow the trail crosses the creek bed several times and comes to a crossing of an old forest road (26.44 mile / 36.48.179N, 91.14.955W). The trail crosses another creek bed then begins a good climb to the trailhead at Forest Road 3152 (27.50 mile / 36.47.576N, 91.15.454W). This trailhead is the southwestern terminus for the Between the Rivers Section and is the northeastern terminus for the Eleven Point River Section. There is plenty of room to turn a horse trailer around in this parking lot.

The Ozark Trail runs along an old railroad bed in Devils Run.

# Trail Notes

_____

_____

_____

_____

_____

_____

_____

_____

_____

_____

_____

_____

_____

_____

_____

_____

_____

_____

_____

_____

_____

_____

_____

_____

_____

_____

_____

_____

_____

On the bank of the Eleven Point River.

# ELEVEN POINT RIVER
## Section

DISTANCE 24.21 MILES
TRAIL USERS foot, bike, horse

## ABOUT THIS SECTION

This is one of the most scenic sections of the Ozark Trail. River views, ridgetops, deep hollows, creeks, springs, caves and McCormack Lake all add to the outstanding natural beauty of this section. Bald eagles and numerous wildflowers are common sights while traveling along this section. The trail passes Bockman Spring, which is a cave with a spring running through it. In the past, area residents used the cave to preserve foods and goods. Many areas of this section of the Ozark Trail will flood during times that the Eleven Point River reaches high water levels.

## HOW TO GET THERE: Trailhead Parking areas

**Forest Road 3152 Trailhead-** Located on Forest Road 3152, 5 miles southwest of the Sinking Creek Lookout Tower Trailhead or from the west, 5 miles from Highway 19. This parking area is large, with enough room to turn a horse trailer around. This is the eastern terminus trailhead.

**Greer Recreation Area and Campground Access-** Located on the east side of Highway 19 at the Eleven Point River, 9 miles north of the city of Alton.

MAPS
USGS Quadrangle maps:
Greer, Piedmont Hollow

CAMPING FACILITIES
Camping is permitted along the trail in USFS lands 100' from the trail.

Greer Crossing Recreation Area-
Primitive campsites, fire pit, vault toilets, open year round, water (in season).

McCormack Lake Recreation Area-
Primitive campsites, fire pit, vault toilets, no water.

NEAREST TOWNS & SERVICES
Alton, Thomasville, West Plains.

**McCormack Lake Trailhead-** Located at the McCormack Lake Recreation Area and Campground. The spur trail to the OT can be accessed from the day-use parking lot at the lake. Located northwest of the Greer Recreation Area, take Highway 19 north 3.81 miles and turn left on Forest Road 3155. Continue on this forest road for 2 miles and the day-use parking area is on the left.

**Forest Road 4155 Trailhead-** North from Thomasville 3.25 miles on State Highway 99, turn right on to County Road 4301 (FR 3173). Continue 1.64 miles and turn left on to Forest Road 4155. Forest Road 4155 is a rough road and may not be drivable in a low clearance vehicle or without four-wheel-drive after a rain. The trailhead is located .73 miles down this forest road. This is the western terminus trailhead.

**Trail Description east to west**
Beginning at the eastern terminus trailhead located on Forest Road 3152 the trail heads downhill for over a mile. There are a few up hills on the descent to the bottom. Travel through an oak and hickory forest with some scattered pine trees. Towards the bottom of the downhill there is a crossing of a creek bed (.96 mile / 36.47.306N, 91.15.975W). Go a short distance to the crossing of Hurricane Creek (1.43 mile / 36.47.064N, 91.16.253W). This is a wide creek and will very likely be wet. The trail will follow down in the bottoms to the upland route and river route split (1.54 mile / 36.47.068N, 91.16.387W). The river route

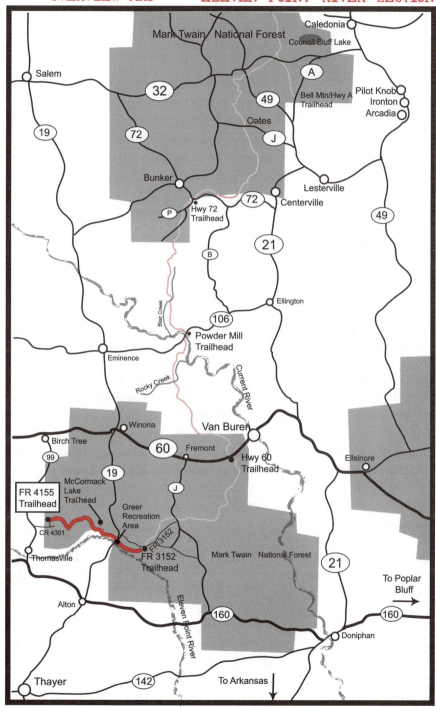

Mark Twain National Forest
Caledonia
Council Bluff Lake
Salem
A
Bell Mtn/Hwy A Trailhead
Pilot Knob
Ironton
Arcadia
32
49
Oates
72
J
Bunker
72
Centerville
Lesterville
P
Hwy 72 Trailhead
19
72
B
21
49
106
Ellington
Blair Creek
Powder Mill Trailhead
Eminence
Rocky Creek
Current River
Winona
Van Buren
Birch Tree
99
60
Fremont
Hwy 60 Trailhead
Ellsinore
19
McCormack Lake Trailhead
J
FR 4155 Trailhead
Greer Recreation Area
CR 4301
FR 3152
Thomasville
FR 3152 Trailhead
Mark Twain National Forest
21
To Poplar Bluff
Alton
Eleven Point River
160
Doniphan
160
Thayer
142
To Arkansas

is the shorter way to go at just 4.3 miles to where the trails rejoin. In comparison, the upland route travels 5.67 miles.

## RIVER ROUTE TRAIL

Continuing on the river route trail, the trail looks like a rocky creek bed, then comes out of the rocky area to an old road. This road surface gives way to a single-track path (1.76 mile / 36.46.953N, 91.16.528W) and soon crosses Hurricane Creek again (1.85 mile / 36.46.896N, 91.16.605W). This will most likely be a wet crossing. The bluish green creek is now along the right side with large bluffs that have cave like formations. In the next .40 mile the trail crosses Hurricane Creek two more times. These crossings will most likely be wet and can be impassable during times of high water levels. The trail begins to turn away from the creek on what used to be a road, and now is overgrown. An old fence and some yucca plants remain from an old homestead. While still on the old road, you'll pass a big round rock on the right side, and the old fence is on the left (2.25 mile / 36.46.611N, 91.16.746W). Pass through an area with a lot of pines. Then, you'll get your first glimpses of the blue green waters of the Eleven Point River and a neat area with rapids.

There's a camp area here (2.52 mile / 36.46.523N, 91.17.036W). Travel along the river and pass another rapids area (2.91 mile / 36.46.672N, 91.17.338W). These rapids areas are referred to as the Mary Deckard Shoals. The next landmark is an old foundation located right next to the trail. The old road heads up the hill and the trail continues along the river and changes to single track. The trail goes through some cane areas along the river. Then turns away from the river going up into some cedars and travels up on a ridge.

For a while you can't see the river and the trail gets really rocky. Then the trail comes down a steep switchback to a creek crossing (3.72 mile / 36.47.211N, 91.17.725W). This crossing can be muddy and tough to get through dry. From here, the trail gets sandy and difficult to follow. Go through more cane and come to a spot right next to the river (4.01 mile / 36.47.154N, 91.18.019W). The trail then goes away from the river and passes a camp spot (4.22 mile / 36.47.129N, 91.18.231W). The trail climbs up on the ridge and through some pine trees. The trail gets rockier towards the top of the hill (4.54 mile / 36.47.144N, 91.18.521W). The trail heads back down on the rocky trail, and near the bottoms crosses a creek bed (4.72 mile/ 36.47.189N, 91.18.635W). For the next .72 miles the trail continues in the bottoms then cuts up on the ridge for a short distance. Then it comes to the junction of the river and upland routes (5.44 mile / 36.47.531N, 91.19.090W).

**UPLAND ROUTE (miles are from the split)**

This route is longer and hillier than the river route, and travels through an upland forest with one great overlook. The upland route as the name suggests, begins with a big climb. The trail climbs switchbacks making the ascent gradual and at one corner there's a nice view of the river below (.60 mile / 36.47.030N, 91.16.630W). Go up and over the top and back around the southeast side of the hilltop. There's a great overlook where you can see the river way out in the distance to the southwest (.94 mile / 36.47.117N, 91.16.613W). Continue slightly uphill and head west along the ridgeline. The trail dips between hillsides and comes to an old forest road with lots of trees down across it (1.38 mile / 36.47.017N, 91.17.059W). Cross the forest road and head downhill. There are a lot of pines and some switchbacks (1.94 mile / 36.47.220N, 91.17.470W).

The trail travels through a dip between hillsides with really big boulders in it. Cross to another dip between hillsides to a spot where the trail goes right next to a huge boulder. The trail begins going down switchbacks through a high glade area with black rocks (2.38 mile / 36.47.415N, 91.17.580W). The trail makes its way to the bottom only to start back up another hill (3.16 mile / 36.47.257N, 91.17.909W). The trail turns west and you can see the river down below. For .25 miles follow along the ridge in the upland forest. The trail then turns away from the river and begins downhill (3.61 mile / 36.47.342N, 91.18.203W). At the bottom in Hackleton Hollow the trail crosses an old forest road (3.87 mile / 36.47.289N, 91.18.313W). The trail then heads uphill again for a little over a half mile to the top (4.56 mile / 36.47.470N, 91.18.484W). Over the next mile the trail makes its way down to the junction with the river route trail.

## TRAIL RE-JOINED

Continue west from the junction (using the mileage via the river route. If you took the upland route add 1.77 miles to the miles noted from here on). From the junction (5.44 mile / 36.47.531N, 91.19.090W) continue on and go toward the Greer Recreation Area and Highway 19. The trail is in the woods without views of the river. A short distance after leaving the junction, the trail crosses an old forest road that is closed (was FR 4029) (5.56 mile / 36.47.612N, 91.19.104W).

Over the next half-mile the trail rolls up and down through Graveyard Hollow and to the crossing of Ross Cemetery Road (6.03 mile / 36.47.580N, 91.19.503W). This road is well traveled and goes out to Highway 19. After crossing Ross Cemetery Road, the trail heads back uphill through some switchbacks and travels along the top of the ridge for a short distance. Then descend the switchbacks. You may catch a view of Greer Recreation Area and Campground through the trees. In the bottoms, on the way to the campground, you'll pass the trail registration box (6.30 mile / 36.47.710N, 91.19.739W). Then it's just a short walk to the campground. The next campground is 3.5 miles farther on the trail located at McCormack Lake Recreation Area.

Note: There is an alternate river route spur trail that leaves Greer Recreation area down by the boat ramp area. This route travels under Highway 19 and follows down in the bottoms near the river before re-joining with the Ozark Trail.

Bluff view of the Eleven Point River.

Bockman Cave and spring.

Continuing on the Ozark Trail from the trail registration box at Greer Recreation Area (6.30 mile / 36.47.710N, 91.19.739W) head west on the trail. It's just .18 mile to the crossing of Highway 19. The trail goes straight across the highway and enters the woods on the other side. This part of the trail stays up on the ridge for the next .83 miles. Then it heads down towards the river and comes to a junction (7.20 mile / 36.48.212N, 91.20.182W). This is the junction of the river route from Greer Recreation Area joining the ridge route. Continuing westward the trail is down in the bottoms along the river and comes to a rather deep ravine creek crossing (7.26 mile / 36.48.262N, 91.20.229W). If you look around there are usually a few different routes down and across here, pick the best one and cross. The trail stays in the bottoms for another .17 miles then begins its climb up to a great picnic area with a great view: this is a definite WOW! spot (7.59 mile / 36.48.492N, 91.20.372W). This spot offers one of the best views on the entire Ozark Trail. Onward and upward through a glade clearing with black rocks and a view, through a section of trail lined with green lichen covered rocks. The trail continues up and around this ridgeline to the next WOW! spot (8.56 mile / 36.48.785N, 91.20.922W). This is another view area with a picnic table. All that climbing was worth it, wasn't it! This is another of the best spots along the Ozark Trail with a view of the Eleven Point River. Head down through some neat terrain to the junction (8.78 mile / 36.48.780N, 91.21.042W) of the spur trail that goes to McCormack Lake Recreation Area and Campground. It is 1.1 miles on the spur trail to McCormack Lake Recreation Area and Campground.

Continuing from the McCormack Lake junction on the Ozark Trail, and the trail comes to a fork in the dirt road (8.90 mile / 36.48.792N, 91.21.128W). Stay to the left. In the springtime these hills are covered with wildflowers. Go a short distance to another intersection and stay to the right (9.15 mile / 36.48.659N, 91.21.319W). This dirt road continues to where the trail turns off to the right (9.43 mile / 36.48.675N, 91.21.615W). The trail is close to the river (9.50 mile / 36.48.723N, 91.21.641W) for about a tenth of a mile until the trail begins to climb up switchbacks (9.60 mile / 36.48.761N, 91.21.563W). Near the top there is a spot with good views of the river. Of course the best views are when there are no leaves on the trees (10.08 mile / 36.49.074N, 91.21.668W).

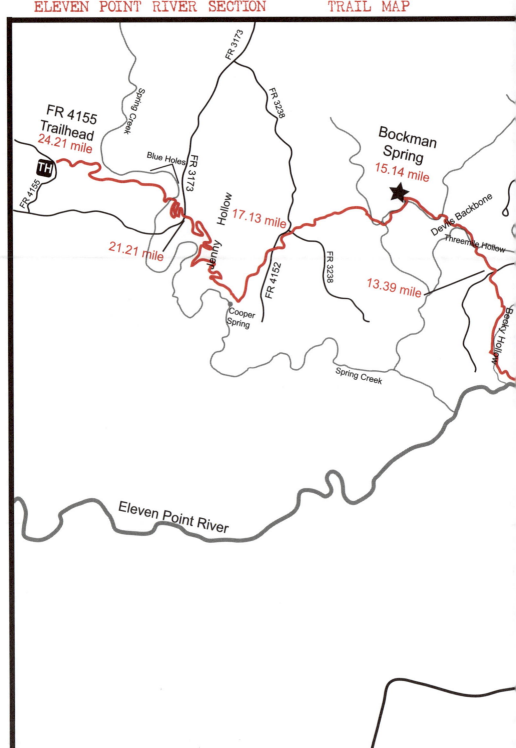

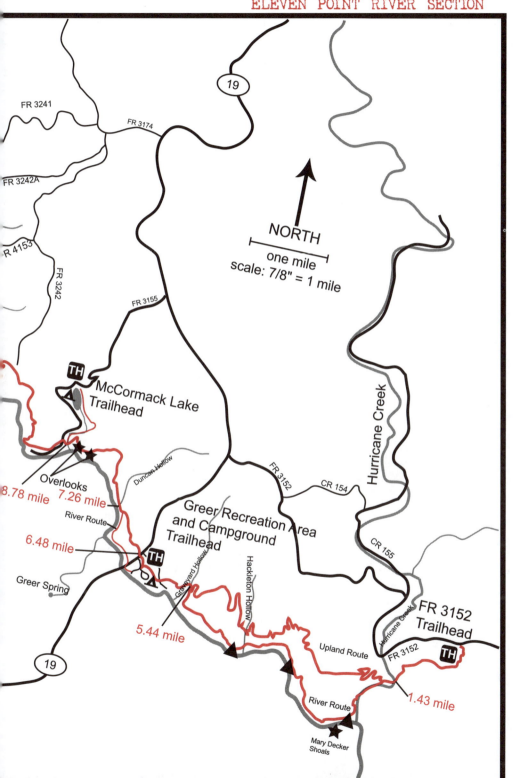

The trail continues up, along and over this ridgeline for the next 1.47 miles, then crosses through some ravines at the bottom. As the OT begins back uphill there is anothr spot with a great view of the river (11.55 mile / 36.49.204N, 91.22.309W). Head back uphill through the switchbacks. The trail begins to turn away from the Eleven Point River.

After crossing over the hill, the trail begins descending into Becky Hollow and comes to a small "no number" forest road crossing (12.16 mile / 36.49.441N, 91.22.743W). On the way out of Becky Hollow the trail crosses three creek beds then crosses another forest road without a number (12.63 mile / 36.49.811N, 91.22.767W). The trail begins to climb up through some areas with some great pine trees. After making it to the top, the trail crosses Forest Road 4153 (13.39 mile / 36.50.299N, 91.22.913W). After crossing the forest road, the trail goes uphill for a short distance before beginning through a switchback descent into Three

The Boot Tree

Mile Hollow where the trail joins with a road (13.87 mile / 36.50.478N, 91.23.217W).

The trail continues on this atv path/road as it climbs up Devils Backbone where the trail goes back to single track through the black rocks (14.44 mile / 36.50.673N, 91.23.695W). The trail comes down from there and turns left onto a rocky road (14.61 mile / 36.50.726N, 91.23.778W). Cross through several rocky creek beds and pass the "boot tree". That's right, "boot tree". It might not still be there but at one time there was a boot on the top of a small tree here (14.74 mile / 36.50.713N, 91.23.873W). Here the OT goes through some grassy areas and a smaller road comes in from the right; stay on the bigger road that you're on. The trail comes to a clearing and on a tree is a sign that says Bockman Spring. The spring is to the right in the rock bluff. It's a narrow cavern that has a spring running through it, a WOW! spot (15.14 mile / 36.50.640N, 91.24.412W). From the spring, the trail is still on the little dirt road and comes to an intersection; stay to the left

The entrance of Bockman Spring.

(15.51 mile / 36.50.640N, 91.24.412W) and at the next intersection, stay to the right (15.68 mile / 36.50.518N, 91.24.467W). Continue on the little dirt road to the next intersection. Stay to the left and then cross a creek bed (15.84 mile / 36.50.546N, 91.24.629W). You'll pass through a large patch of prickly pear cactus here. A road comes in on the left (16.14 mile / 36.50.633N, 91.24.858W). Stay on the same road you've been on. Keep your eyes open for where the trail turns off the road. It's a difficult spot to see where the trail cuts back up to the trees (16.39 mile / 36.50.537N, 91.25.091W). The trail makes its way up to the crossing of Forest Road 3238 (17.13 mile / 36.50.231N, 91.25.636W).

The trail crosses FR 3238 and continues in the forest and climbs to the crossing of Forest Road 4152 (17.57 mile / 36.50.013N, 91.25.842W). Descend, then climb again to another forest road crossing (18.09 mile / 36.49.670N, 91.26.105W). The trail makes its way along this ridge that has some great pine tree areas. The OT gets rocky here and there is a spot where you can see the very blue colored water of Cooper Spring far down below (18.53 mile / 36.49.496N, 91.26.276W). The trail begins to descend towards Jenny Hollow and makes a northernly bend heading away from the ridge (18.63 mile / 36.49.562N, 91.26.382W). Continue down through switchbacks to Jenny Hollow. The trail crosses a forest road with no number (19.27 mile / 36.49.711N, 91.26.605W). The trail climbs up out of Jenny Hollow and comes to a confusing "T" intersection; go to the right here (19.68 mile / 36.49.689N, 91.26.851W). After going somewhat downhill, the trail will begin a climb up to a pine and oak tree "knob" area (19.93 mile / 36.49.893N, 91.26.785W). Then the trail descends through switchbacks, returns to the hollow, and comes to a forest road (20.33 mile / 36.49.986N, 91.26.662W). Follow the road to the left for 10-15', and then the trail goes back into the woods to the right. Go a short distance to the bottoms. There is a little creek bed that runs parallel to the trail on the right (20.42 mile / 36.50.040N, 91.26.712W). The next .67 miles is mostly uphill and the trail comes to a confusing spot where there is a forest road just to the left of the trail (21.09 mile / 36.50.114N, 91.26.965W). Be attentive here to stay on the trail and not the road. From here it's just a short distance to the crossing of Forest Road 3173 (21.21 mile / 36.50.188N, 91.27.055W).

Through the cedars on the Eleven Point River Section.

ELEVEN POINT RIVER SECTION

From FR 3173, the trail heads downhill .75 miles on some very long switchbacks, to the crossing of Spring Creek (22.06 mile / 36.50.308N, 91.27.235W). To the right of here down the creek are two very blue pools (blue holes). The crossing of Spring Creek can be dry much of the year. After crossing the creek bed the trail goes up to a grassy field and a dirt/grass road(22.09 mile / 36.50.326N, 91.27.278W). Pay very close attention here, the trail cuts off this road to the left through an area that gets overgrown by briars and grasses. To make it even more difficult, the trail marker here often gets knocked down or taken down. Once you've made your way through the briars and grasses the trail begins up the hill and climbs the ridge for .25 miles to where it crosses a forest road with no number (22.27 mile / 36.50.418N, 91.27.431W). The trail continues the next 1.94 miles along the ridge. At times the trail gets extremely rocky and narrow. Make the descent off of the ridge to the trailhead located on FR 4155 (24.21 mile / 36.50.460N, 91.28.908W). Note: Forest Road 4155 can be extremely rough and a high clearance vehicle may be necessary. This is the western terminus of the Eleven Point River Section of the Ozark Trail.

# Trail Notes

View of the North Fork River.

# NORTH FORK
## Section

DISTANCE 26.68 MILES
(Northern 11 miles are currently in bad shape)
TRAIL USERS foot, bike, horse
Foot Traffic only in the Devils Backbone Wilderness Area

## ABOUT THIS SECTION

This section hasn't gotten much publicity in the past. Due to minimal use and inconsistent maintenance the northern 11 miles of this section are currently in bad shape. These northern miles are in serious need of maintenance and marking. In areas the trail just cannot be followed. This is a great opportunity for someone or a group to adopt this section of trail to do the needed maintenance.

The good news is that the remaining 15.68 miles make for a great hike or ride. This section doesn't have too many climbs and a lot of the trail is wide and is on what looks like were old forest roads. There are only a few places that need a little work. The Ozark Trail is only open to hikers in the Devils Backbone Wilderness Area. This section travels past springs, a cave and a scenic river-front area that makes for a good place to have lunch.

## HOW TO GET THERE: Trailhead Parking areas

**Blue Hole Trailhead-** Located on State Highway AP, northwest of the city of West Plains. From U.S. Highway 63 go west on State Highway 14, 9 miles and turn right (north) on State Highway AP. Continue 10 miles and the trailhead is located on the right.

## MAPS
USGS Quadrangle maps:
Pomona, Siloam Springs,
Dora, Cureall NW
If traveling only from the
Blue Hole Trailhead to
the Collins Ridge Road
Trail head only Siloam
Springs, Dora and
Cureall NW are
necessary.

## CAMPING FACILITIES
Camping is permitted
along the trail in USFS
lands 100' from the trail.

North Fork Recreation
Area (Hammond Mill)
Primitive campsites, fire
ring, table, vault toilets,
water (seasonal).
Open May 15 through
December 5.

## NEAREST TOWNS & SERVICES
Pomona, West Plains.

**McGarr Ridge Trailhead-** Located 14 miles west of West Plains on State Highway CC. From the Blue Hole Trailhead take AP south and turn right (west) on 14. Turn left (south) on Highway T. At Siloam Springs turn left (south) on County Road 103 and at the intersection with State Highway CC turn right (west). The trailhead is 2.5 miles on CC.

**Collins Ridge Trailhead-** Located south of the McGarr Ridge Trailhead on County Road 362. From the McGarr Ridge Trailhead take State Highway CC east 4 miles and turn right on State Highway AD. Stay on AD for 3 miles and turn right (west) on State Highway KK. Travel 2.5 miles and turn right on County Road 362. The trailhead is located 1.5 miles down County Road 362.

## Trail Description North to South

Currently the Forest Service does not recommend traveling the northern 11 miles from Pomona to the Blue Hole Trailhead. This trail description and mileage begins at the Blue Hole Trailhead located on State Highway AP, 1.78 miles north of State Highway 14. The trailhead (36.50.092N, 92.03.177W) is on the western side of the highway. The trailhead is currently in poor condition, and is on the list for Forest Service renovations. Begin at the parking area and the Ozark Trail heads west on an old paved section of trail. Shortly the trail cuts off to the right on a dirt path (that shows signs of ATV use) and goes down hill. Continue .45 miles to where the trail turns left off of the

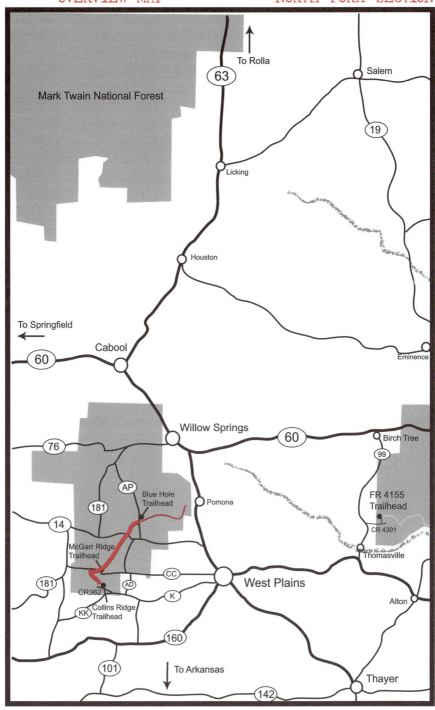

To Rolla

63

Mark Twain National Forest

Salem

19

Licking

Houston

To Springfield

Cabool

60

Eminence

Willow Springs

60

76

Birch Tree

99

AP

Blue Hole Trailhead

181

Pomona

FR 4155 Trailhead

14

CR 4301

McGarr Ridge Trailhead

Thomasville

181

CR362

CC

AD

West Plains

K

Alton

KK

Collins Ridge Trailhead

160

101

To Arkansas

Thayer

142

Possible Day Trips
Blue Hole Trailhead to
McGarr Ridge Trailhead
9.65 miles (one-way).

McGarr Ridge Trailhead
to Collins Ridge
Trailhead 6 miles (one-way).

Contacts
US Forest Service
Ava/Willow Springs
District Office
1103 S. Jefferson
Ava, MO 65608
417-683-4428

wider path and heads up the hill (.55 mile / 36.50.134N, 92.03.517W). Ascend to the top of the hill to the field. The trail goes through this clearing and re-enters the woods next to a large pine tree (.77 mile / 36.50.001N, 92.03.555W). This spot can get overgrown. At the bottom of the descent, cross a creek bed (1.00 mile / 36.50.053N, 92.03.785W) and the trail continues in the bottoms. Use caution here, as this area gets overgrown and can be difficult to follow.

The trail turns left (1.19 mile / 36.50.051N, 92.03.968W) and goes up the hill. Pay close attention here, as this is another spot that is easy to miss. The trail climbs and goes through an area that had a fire (1.41 mile / 36.49.891N, 92.04.078W). This area is overgrown with small trees. Cross through a small creek bed (1.69 mile / 36.49.680N, 92.03.992W) and go up hill. The OT is not over grown with trees after this crossing. At mile 2.45 the trail crosses Forest Road 794. Continue to a clearing that is being used as a dump (2.94 mile / 36.49.164N, 92.04.563W). Watch closely here. It is easy to miss the trail markers and they are frequently missing. The trail is difficult to follow the short distance to State Highway 14. It comes to a sign marking the directions to Tabor Creek, North Fork, Dry Creek, Horton, and Noblett (3.00 mile / 36.49.137N, 92.04.638W).

At State Highway 14 the trail goes straight across and past some nice pine trees. Pass an old trash dump, complete with a blue truck fender, and then go past a camp area(3.51 mile / 36.48.758N, 92.04.732W). Over the next .70 miles the trail gets a bit sketchy and difficult to follow. There is not much of a trail path in here, so keep your eyes open for silver diamond markers and green and white OT markers. At mile 3.85, cross a forest road (36.48.592N, 92.04.977W). The trail goes straight across and gradually descends to a rocky area that looks like it may have been a mine or quarry (5.32 miles / 36.47.796N, 92.06.002W). The descent steepens and the trail goes through some switchbacks. At the bottom, cross a dirt road (5.51 mile / 36.47.795N, 92.06.094W). If you are in need of water turn right at this road and go about .50 miles to a spring fed creek. This road also leads to an area that is used to camp at Braddock Lake.

Continue from the dirt road, go straight across and through the walnut grove, to the crossing of Tabor Creek (5.64 mile / 36.47.713N, 92.06.198W). This creek bed is usually dry, but after a good rain this can be a dangerous crossing. There are numerous fragrant Witch Hazel bushes in the creek bed. Witch Hazel's yellow flowers bloom in late winter. From the creek bed the trail follows an old road, but quickly turns to the left off the old road (5.67 mile / 36.47.725N, 92.06.210W). The old road continues straight. The trail climbs up and crosses a gravel road (5.93 mile / 36.47.581N, 92.06.348W). Continue up the hill on the trail. The trail gets steeper towards the top of the ridge, and on top of the ridge the trail parallels Tabor Creek, which is far below to the left. This ridge is nice with neat rocks and some pine trees. Below the ridge, Tabor Cave hides in the steep hillside. Continue on the OT to the sign for the

**Ozark Witch Hazel is a native Missouri shrub that grows in gravel creek beds. The yellow and red fragrant flowers bloom in the late winter.**

Spring Creek

Dry Creek

Burn Area

TH Blue Hole Trailhead

2.45 mile

14

FR 749

Dump

AP

3.51 mile

FR 795

Spring

Braddock Lake

Mine Hollow

Tabor Creek

5.51 mile

Trail Camp

6.35 mile

Tabor Creek

McGarr Ridge Highway CC Trailhead

TH

9.65 mile

North Fork Campground

Blue Spring

Devils Backbone Wilderness Area Foot traffic only from this to Collins Ridge Trailhead

CC

Scenic River view

12.63 mile

11.52 mile

McGarr Ridge

Crooked Creek

Land Survey Marker

TH Collins Ridge Trailhead

15.68 mile

To Highway KK

CR 362

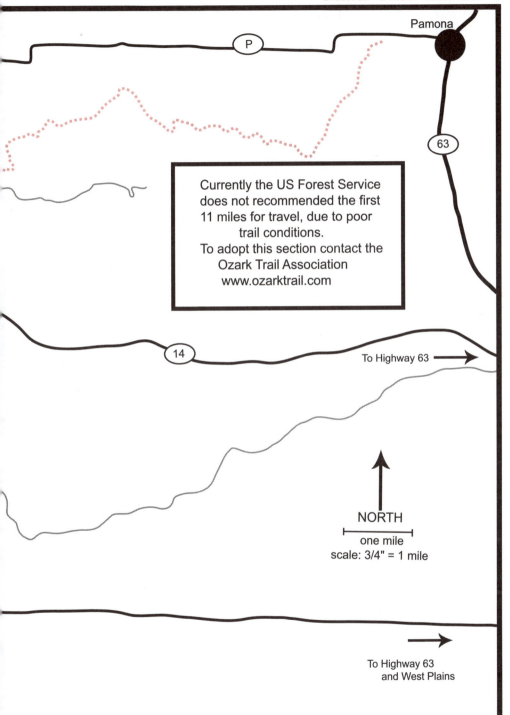

Pamona

P

63

Currently the US Forest Service does not recommended the first 11 miles for travel, due to poor trail conditions.
To adopt this section contact the Ozark Trail Association
www.ozarktrail.com

14

To Highway 63 →

NORTH

one mile
scale: 3/4" = 1 mile

→

To Highway 63
and West Plains

"Trail Camp" (6.35 mile / 36.47.268N, 92.06.467W). This is a nice camp area that also has a small metal fire grate. A short distance from here the trail crosses an old forest road (6.44 mile / 36.47.248N, 92.06.477W). At mile 6.47 another trail intersects, and the Ozark Trail goes to the left (36.47.244N, 92.06.497W). The OT crosses an old dirt road at mile 7.07 (36.46.913N, 92.06.709W). Continue on to another old dirt road crossing (7.69 mile / 36.46.502N, 92.06.645W). Down to the right there is a wildlife pond and a nice stand of pines. At the next old dirt road (8.37 mile / 36.46.236N, 92.07.227W) turn left. The OT follows this old road past a wildlife pond. Another dirt road (8.75 mile / 36.45.923W, 92.07.160W) comes in from the right. Continue on the wide path to the left (not really a turn, just continuing in the direction you have been going). At mile 8.90 a wide path forks in from the left; continue to the right (36.45.704N, 92.07.635W). The OT continues as this wide path to the Trailhead parking area located on State Highway CC (9.65 mile / 36.45.733N, 92.07.881W). There is plenty of room to turn a horse trailer around in this parking area.

Across State Highway CC you will find the trail registration box (9.77 mile / 36.45.668N, 92.07.894W). This is one of the nicest registration boxes on the OT. The trail is now in the Devil's Backbone Wilderness Area and only hikers are allowed on the trail south of this point. Horse and bike traffic are not permitted. The trail is pretty wide. Continue to the fork and go to the right (10.40 mile / 36.45.147N, 92.07.981W). The trail traverses McGarr Ridge to the cut off for the spur trail that leads to Blue Spring and the North Fork Campground (11.52 mile / 36.44.742N, 92.08.936W). To go to the spring and the campground turn right here and the side trip is about .70 mile, one-way. Continue on the Ozark Trail and the trail descends, first gradually then steeper to a point where the trail forks (12.63 mile / 36.44.619N, 92.10.046W). To the right .10 mile is a camp area near the bank of the North Fork River. This is a great spot with a scenic bluff across the river. We saw three eagles here on an early spring hike. Continue from the point of the split to the left and the OT crosses Crooked Creek (13.23 mile / 36.44.512N, 92.10.019W).

The trail goes uphill from Crooked Creek, to where an old road goes off to the left, stay to the right on the old road/trail and up the hill. At the 13.36 mile point the OT comes to a fork, go left

A trail marker melted by a forest fire.

and up the hill (36.44.492N, 92.10.087W).  Continue nearly a mile to another fork (14.34 mile / 36.43.874N, 92.09.624W). Continue to the left.  The trail passes through a very nice stand of pines, to a clearing, then back into the woods to a point where an old road cuts off to the left.  Continue straight on the OT (14.62 mile / 36.43.731N, 92.09.392W).  The trail passes a land survey marker (15.11 mile / 36.43.405N, 92.09.093W), then shortly comes to a point where another trail goes off to the right (15.15 mile / 36.43.400N, 92.09.053W).  Continue straight on the OT.  In .15 miles, a trail comes in from the left side (15.31 mile / 36.43.396N, 92.08.889W).  Continue straight on the Ozark Trail.  In .3 miles, another old road goes to the left (15.60 mile / 36.43.225N, 92.08.672W). Stay on the small single-track trail that goes straight and leads to the Collins Ridge Road Trailhead parking area (15.68 mile / 36.43.164N, 92.08.683W).  This is the southern terminus of the North Fork Section of the Ozark Trail.

# Trail Notes

Deb Ridgway and Margo Carroll hiking through
Devil's Tollgate.

# TAUM SAUK
## Section

DISTANCE 32.85 MILES
TRAIL USERS foot traffic only

## ABOUT THIS SECTION

This is the most traveled section of the Ozark Trail for hikers (Courtois is probably the most used for mountain bikers and Wapappello and Victory for equestrians). The description of the trail on this section has been divided into three sections and each is described in the direction that most hikers take. There are outstanding rock formations, great views, a waterfall, a look out tower, Johnson Shut-Ins and the highest point in the state of Missouri. Note that Johnson's Shut-Ins State Park gets very busy on nice days and there is a limit to how many visitors may enter the park. Be prepared to wait to get in and if you plan on camping at Johnson's Shut-Ins State Park be sure to make reservations.

A store is located at Johnson's Shut-Ins State Park and is open Memorial Day through Labor Day weekend, 8 a.m. to 8 p.m. During the months of April and May the store is open a limited amount of hours and it is closed November through March.

The nearby towns of Arcadia and Caledonia feature restaurants and services. After a rugged hike on this section, stopping for a meal at one of the local restaurants makes for a satisfying treat. The Arcadian Valley, surrounded by the St. Francis Mountains is exceptionally beautiful. Elephant Rocks State Park is close by. This park features unique huge boulders and an

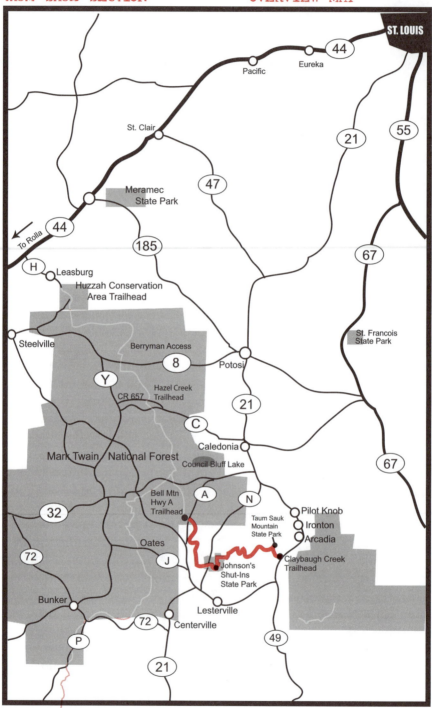

ST. LOUIS

44

Pacific

Eureka

44

St. Clair

21

55

47

Meramec
State Park

185

67

To Rolla    44

H    Leasburg
Huzzah Conservation
Area Trailhead

Steelville

Berryman Access

St. Francois
State Park

8    Potosi

Y

CR 657    Hazel Creek
Trailhead

C

21

Caledonia

Mark Twain  National Forest

Council Bluff Lake

Bell Mtn
Hwy A
Trailhead    A

N

67

Pilot Knob

Taum Sauk
Mountain
State Park    Ironton

32

Arcadia

Oates

Claybaugh Creek
Trailhead

72

J

Johnson's
Shut-Ins
State Park

Bunker

P

72

Lesterville

Centerville

49

21

interpretive trail. Although not part of the Ozark Trail, this park makes for an enjoyable trip.

## HOW TO GET THERE: Trailhead Parking areas

**Claybaugh Creek Trailhead-** Located on Highway 21, 5 miles south of Arcadia. The trailhead is located on the right.

**Taum Sauk Mountain State Park Trailhead-** Located off Highway 21, south of Arcadia on Highway CC. From Arcadia drive south 4 miles on Highway 21, and turn right (west) on State Highway CC. Continue on State Highway CC for 3.5 miles and to the large parking area and trailhead.

**Johnson's Shut-Ins State Park Trailhead-** From Highway 21 at Graniteville, turn southwest on State Highway N. Stay on N for 13.5 miles and turn left on Taum Sauk Trail Road. Continue on this road .75 miles to the large parking area located near the park store.

**Highway A / Bell Mountain Wilderness Trailhead-** Located southwest from the city of Caledonia. From Caledonia take Highway 21 south 4 miles and turn right (west) on State Highway 32. Travel 7 miles on State Highway 32 and turn left (south) on State Highway A. Continue on A for 5.3 miles and the trailhead is on the right.

USGS Quadrangle maps: Johnson Mountain, Edgehill, Johnson's Shut Ins, Ironton

CAMPING FACILITIES
Camping is permitted along the trail in USFS and DNR lands 100' from the trail. Camping is not allowed 2 miles east or west of Johnson's Shut-Ins State Park main parking lot.

Taum Sauk Mountain State Park Campground- Camping, fire pit, vault toilets, water (in season) Johnson's Shut-Ins State Park Campground- Camping, fire pit, toilets, showers, water (in season), store.

NEAREST TOWNS & SERVICES
Arcadia, Ironton, Caledonia.

The Chocolate Garage in Caledonia is a popular stop after hiking.

Johnson's Shut-Ins State Park-Store offers a limited supply of groceries and items. Open Memorial Day weekend through Labor Day weekend 8am-8pm, April and May limited hours, and closed November through March.

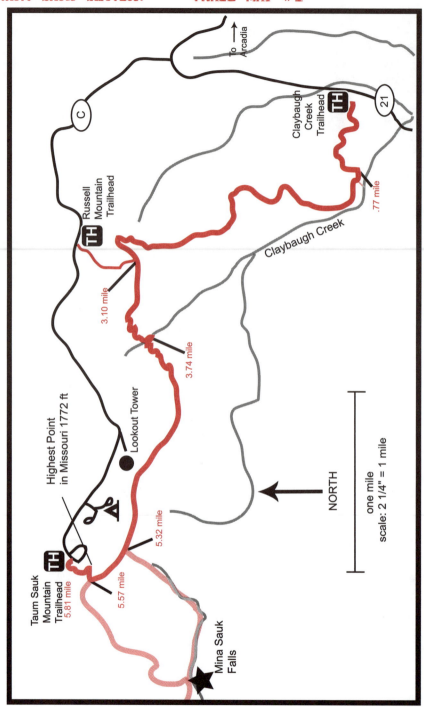

To
Arcadia

C

21

Claybaugh Creek Trailhead

.77 mile

Russell Mountain Trailhead

Claybaugh Creek

3.10 mile

3.74 mile

Lookout Tower

Highest Point in Missouri 1772 ft

NORTH

one mile
scale: 2 1/4" = 1 mile

5.32 mile

Taum Sauk Mountain Trailhead

5.81 mile

5.57 mile

Mina Sauk Falls

## Trail Description Claybaugh Creek Trailhead to Taum Sauk Mountain Park 5.81 miles (Taum Sauk map #1)

Start at the Claybaugh Creek Trailhead parking lot (37.32.939N, 90.40.786W) and travel up through an oak and hickory forest in the Claybaugh Creek watershed. The trail immediately goes into the woods and begins the upwards climb to the highest point in Missouri. There is a registration box just into the woods. Cross a little wooden bridge over a small ravine, and the trail begins to level out (.20 mile / 37.32.959N, 90.40.916W). After the trail levels, it rolls up and down somewhat and gains elevation. The trail crosses a little ravine and continues gaining elevation but is not too steep. From here the trail goes downhill (.52 mile / 37.33.018N, 90.41.132W) towards Claybaugh Creek. This oak and hickory covered hillside also has a few scattered pine trees. If the creek has water in it you should be able to hear it soon. This part of the trail has green moss growing along the side. Claybaugh Creek is on the left (.77 mile / 37.32.898N, 90.41.268W). The trail travels along an old dirt road, and comes to a turn(.85 mile / 37.32.904N, 90.41.336W). Watch closely here for where the trail turns right off the old road. The trail continues up the hill on single track. Before turning right and going up the hill you can make a

Possible Day Trips
Claybaugh Trailhead to Taum Sauk Mountain State Park 5.5 miles (one-way).

Taum Sauk Mountain State Park to Mina Sauk Falls 5 miles (round trip).

Bell Mountain Trailhead to Johnson's Shut-Ins State Park 14.70 miles (one-way).

Taum Sauk Mountain Trailhead to Johnson's Shut-Ins State Park 12.60 miles (one-way).

Contacts
Department of Natural Resources Division of State Parks
P.O. Box 176
Jefferson City, MO 65102
(800) 334-6946
www.mostateparks.com

US Forest Service
Potosi Office
Highway 8 West
Potosi, MO 63664
573-468-5427

Missouri Dept. of Conservation
P.O. Box 180
Jefferson City, MO 65102
573-751-4115

side trip down to Claybaugh Creek. This Creek eventually flows down in to the Royal Gorge shut-ins area near Highway 21.

After the turn at the creek the trail continues its gradual gain of altitude. You will find a neat area with rock formations and more pines (WOW! spot )(.99 mile / 37.32.924N, 90.41.374W). Continue uphill. The trail enters a glade area (1.19 mile / 37.33.038N, 90.41.488W) with rock outcroppings, yellow tickseed coreopsis and other flowers. Keep your eyes open for lizards (in warm seasons). The trail returns to the shade of the forest. Cross an old forest road and continue straight across on single track (1.63 mile / 37.33.311N, 90.41.439W). The trail continues to climb. The trail comes to a tricky spot (2.36 mile / 37.33.705N, 90.41.656W). Keep your eyes open here for this bend. From a large flat rock here, the trail goes to the left. Piles of rocks (cairns), and spray paint on the rocks mark this turn. As the OT continues up, it goes through a glade area. After the glade area the trail crosses a rocky ravine and continues climbing. The trail curves, ascending and passes some large rocks similar to the ones at Elephant Rocks State Park. The junction to cut over to the Russell Mountain Trailhead is at 3.10 miles (37.34.034N, 90.41.834W). The Russell Mountain Trailhead is located .46 miles down this connector trail.

Continue on the OT towards the top of Taum Sauk Mountain to a large glade area, WOW! spot (3.37 mile / 37.34.047N, 90.42.113W). There is a nice view. Please take extra care to stay on the trail through this area and other glade areas. Glades are very sensitive ecosystems and are easily destroyed. Watch for Collared Lizards. At 3.39 miles cross a forest road (37.34.067N, 90.42.154W). The trail goes straight across. A sign nailed to a tree says Mirkwood Forest. The trail curves downhill, passes through a small glade opening and goes back into the trees. The downhill steepens and the trail crosses Claybaugh Creek (3.74 mile / 37.33.961N, 90.42.308W).

After the creek, the trail heads back uphill and gets very rocky and steep. In the next mile the trail crosses or skirts along six more glade areas, then crosses a forest road (4.77 mile / 37.33.974N, 90.43.102W). The trail continues in the forest, crosses another glade, then reaches a split. There are two choices here.

Turn left to Mina Sauk Falls and the rest of the Taum Sauk Section, or turn right to Taum Sauk Mountain State Park and the highest point in Missouri (1772'). To go to Taum Sauk Mountain State Park turn to the right and follow the trail about .42 miles to the park. You will come to another split that goes to Mina Sauk Falls, but stay to the right towards the park. This trail changes to a paved trail and passes the highest point in Missouri. The high point is marked with a large boulder and a plaque. The park has camping, and water is available in season.

**The Eastern Collared Lizard is very colorful and has a rather long tail. Females are less colorful, but also have the dark "collared" markings around the neck. The nickname for this glade lizard is mountain boomer.**

The rocky terrain of the Taum Sauk Section.

### Trail Description Taum Sauk Mountain Park Trailhead to Johnson's Shut-Ins State Park 12.60 miles (Taum Sauk map #2)

This is the most hiked section of the Ozark Trail. Starting at the parking lot (37.34.383N, 90.43.736W) follow the paved trail past the highest point to the dirt trail. This section of the trail is some of the rockiest any hiker will ever experience, and can be an ankle twister! A loop trail goes to Mina Sauk Falls and will turn off to the right. Stay to the left to continue to where the trail splits again. This is marked by a sign. To the left are the trailheads at Russell Mountain and Claybaugh Creek. To the right, the trail goes to Mina Sauk Falls (.42 mile / 37.33.974N, 90.43.102W). Continue on the OT towards Mina Sauk Falls and Johnson's Shut-Ins State Park. Follow along the very rocky trail with a little creek that runs along the left side. If this creek has water in it then there will probably be water going over Mina Sauk Falls. In little less than a mile and you will be standing at the top of the falls (1.30 mile / 37.33.750N, 90.44.336W) WOW! spot.

Mina Sauk falls is the tallest waterfall in Missouri, and is a "wet season" waterfall, meaning that water only flows after rains or snow melts. Descend down the trail on the right side of the falls and at the bottom the trail crosses the creek. The trail is not as rocky after crossing below the falls. The trail follows the creek through the woods to an old road crossing (2.07 mile / 37.33.386N, 90.44.779W). Here you will find a good camp area. Go a short

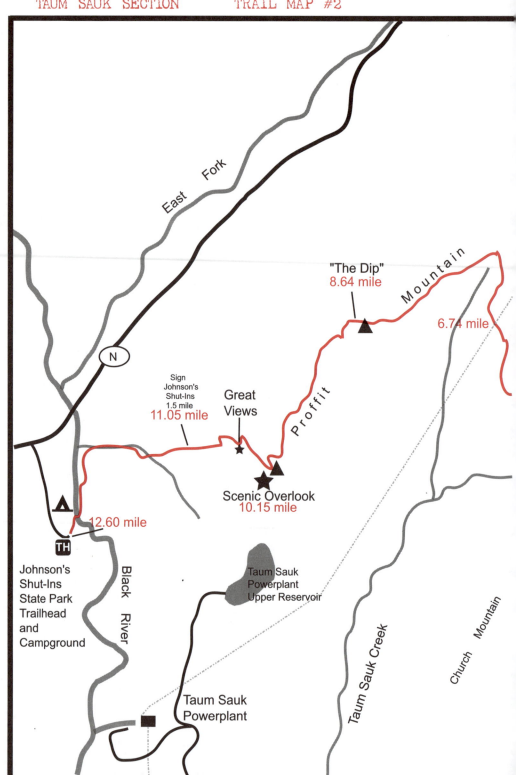

"The Dip"
8.64 mile

Mountain

6.74 mile

East Fork

N

Sign
Johnson's
Shut-Ins
1.5 mile
11.05 mile

Great
Views

Proffit

Scenic Overlook
10.15 mile

12.60 mile

Johnson's
Shut-Ins
State Park
Trailhead
and
Campground

TH

Black River

Taum Sauk
Powerplant
Upper Reservoir

Taum Sauk Creek

Church Mountain

Taum Sauk
Powerplant

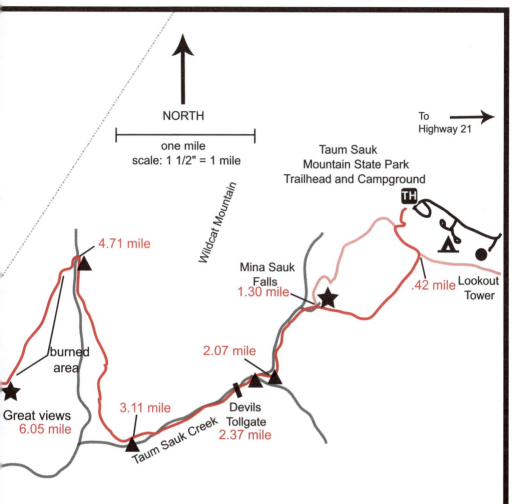

NORTH

one mile
scale: 1 1/2" = 1 mile

To
Highway 21

Taum Sauk
Mountain State Park
Trailhead and Campground

TH

Lookout
Tower
.42 mile

4.71 mile

Wildcat Mountain

Mina Sauk
Falls
1.30 mile

2.07 mile

burned
area

3.11 mile

Devils
Tollgate
2.37 mile

Taum Sauk Creek

Great views
6.05 mile

# Taum Sauk
# Map #2

distance to a creek crossing (2.30 mile, 37.33.319N, 90.44.968W) with a good camping spot near the creek. From here it's a short walk to Devils Tollgate (2.37 mile, 37.33.285N, 90.45.029W). This is a massive rhyolite rock formation that the trail passes through.

Mina Sauk Falls

This is a definite WOW! spot. The trail crosses several little rocky creek areas that are dry most of the year. Then the trail turns right off the old road it has been following (this turn is easy to miss! 3.11 mile / 37.32.985N, 90.45.731W). The trail passes another good camp area (3.39 mile / 37.32.934N, 90.45.977W). The trail follows a ridge as it heads away from the creek, passes an interesting rock shelf, a stand of pine trees and more rock shelves. The trail starts uphill and continues its gradual climb for the next .71 miles. Cross over several little rocky ravines between the ridges to a point with pine trees (4.47 mile / 37.33.688N, 90.46.269W). This is a pretty spot. From here, begin downhill to the next creek crossing (4.71 mile / 37.33.887N, 90.46.365W).

Just before the creek is another good camp area. Past that point, the trail enters an area of forest burned several years ago. The area stretches nearly a mile and can get very warm in summer because of the lack of shade. At 5.92 miles, the trail crests the top of the mountain (37.33.381N, 90.46.859). This is the third highest point on this section. The trail begins a short-lived downhill and comes to an area with great views WOW! spot (6.05 mile / 37.33.288N, 90.46.935W). Go a short distance and cross a rough old road (6.47 mile / 37.33.529N, 90.47.091W). Continue on to the power lines (6.74 mile / 37.33.709N, 90.47.152W). From the powerlines, looking southwest, you can see the upper reservoir of the Taum Sauk Hydroelectric power plant. The reservoir looks like a giant swimming pool on top of a flat-topped mountain. The trail makes its way along the side of Proffit Mountain, crossing some neat clearings with big granite/rhyolite boulders and to another spot with a great view (7.71 mile / 37.34.037N, 90.47.440W). The trail is generally flat here, with a few ups and downs. Go past a good camp area (8.59 mile / 37.33.738N, 90.48.233W) and then on to an area (8.64 mile / 37.33.747N, 90.48.292W) affectionately called "the dip". This spot marks the beginning of the last big climb to the top of Proffit Mountain.

The trail climbs the next .76 miles to the second highest point of this section at 1644 ft.(9.40 mile / 37.33.280N, 90.48.659W). Head downhill. The trail passes a camp area and then (10.14 mile / 37.32.822N, 90.48.981W) to a WOW! spot that has rock outcroppings and great views (10.65 mile / 37.33.023N, 90.49.339W). Still on the descent, you'll pass a sign that says "Johnson's Shut Ins State Park 1.5 miles" (11.05 mile / 37.32.959N, 90.49.654W). The downhill becomes less steep as you reach an area between two ridges where the trail crosses back over a creek three times. Soon you'll see the East Fork of the Black River. The trail parallels the river before crossing it at the small bridge. The bridge is a pedestrian bridge across the river and in the past has been washed out with heavy rains. The bridge is cleverly designed to wash out in heavy rains when logs and debris stack up against it, preventing the bridge from being permanently damaged. Welcome to Johnson's Shut-Ins State Park!

## Trail Description Highway A Bell Mountain Wilderness Trailhead to Johnson's Shut-Ins State Park 14.70 miles (Taum Sauk map #3)

Begin at the Bell Mountain Wilderness Trailhead located on Highway A (0 mile / 37.37.557N, 90.54.652W). From the parking lot cross Highway A. The trail enters the woods on the east side of the road. Immediately, the trail begins a steep half-mile climb up Bell Mountain. This climb is one of four steep climbs on the way over to Johnson's Shut-Ins State Park. After the initial climb, the trail travels 3.5 miles through what many consider to be the best area for scenic viewpoints on the Ozark Trail. In this short distance are five WOW! spots. In just under a mile you are rewarded with the first WOW! spot. This is a nice glade-overlook area (.85 mile / 37.37.366N, 90.54.218W). Then it's just a short walk to the next glade area with another great view (1.28 mile / 37.37.106N, 90.54.161W). The next WOW! spots, all with great views, are located at (1.43 mile / 37.37.011N, 90.54.098W), (2.80 mile / 37.36.261N, 90.53.806W), (2.86 mile / 37.36.214N, 90.53.830W), (3.15 mile / 37.36.014N, 90.53.744W). You'll also pass the cut off to the Bell Mountain Wilderness Area Trail (1.82 mile / 37.36.851N, 90.53.984W). Continue on the OT to the high point, 1,478 ft. (4.04 mile / 37.35.346N, 90.54.181W).

From here the trail goes downhill, crosses through several more glade clearings to another WOW! spot with a great view (4.50 mile / 37.35.142N, 90.54.567W). Watch for stacks of rocks (cairns)

Hiking through a mountain top glade.

used to mark the trail location through the glade areas. The trail comes to another area with a great view of Goggins Mountain (5.05 mile / 37.34.707N, 90.54.424W). The trail continues downhill through rocky glades mixed with trees to the wet crossing of Padfield branch (5.41 mile / 37.34.580N, 90.54.095W). Follow the trail to the old house that's fallen down. Behind the house there is a small spring (5.44 mile / 37.34.569N, 90.54.058W). The trail continues on the old road before turning right (5.87 mile / 37.34.733N, 90.53.661W). Head into the trees, and begin the climb up Goggins Mountain. The trail reaches the top of a ridge and heads back down a short distance before heading back uphill. It comes to a glade opening with a nice view (6.42 mile / 37.34.552N, 90.53.392W). The trail continues going through glades, then trees, as it travels along Goggins Mountain for the next half mile. Then the trail descends and crosses a dirt road (7.26 mile / 37.33.972N, 90.53.714W).

The descent continues through an area with large rocks, and to a glade area (7.53 mile / 37.33.831N, 90.53.878W) where the trail begins back uphill. The trail comes to yet another wonderful WOW! spot with a great view (7.72 mile / 37.33.667N, 90.53.859W). The trail winds up through the glade areas and then wooded areas to a good camp area (8.08 mile / 37.33.430N, 90.53.714W). A short distance from here the trail begins a .30 mile downhill. This doesn't last long and the trail levels out somewhat before beginning back up and crossing a rocky jeep road (9.21 mile / 37.32.517N, 90.53.619W). The trail goes through a glade area and heads back down to another great view point (9.71 mile / 37.32.170N, 90.53.585W). It crosses two old dirt roads (the first one 9.80 mile / 37.32.078N, 90.53.565W), (the second 10.00 mile / 37.31.938N, 90.53.433W).

The scenery changes to more woods and fewer glades as the trail descends from Goggins Mountain. The trail crosses an old road (10.08 mile / 37.31.930N, 90.53.376W) and heads to Walker Branch (10.38 mile / 37.31.894N, 90.53.093W), which is usually dry. The trail crosses the creek and travels up and down, gaining some elevation, and reaches the power lines (10.57 mile / 37.31.927N, 90.52.942W). The power lines carry electricity from the nearby Taum Sauk Hydroelectric Power Plant to St. Louis. The trail makes its way to an old road that has some small trees growing on it (10.83 mile / 37.31.856N, 90.52.709W). The trail is cut into the hillside and continues down past the sign marking the State Park boundary (11.30 mile / 37.31.984N, 90.52.312W). The trail crosses through a rocky creek bed down into the bottoms. In a short distance the OT crosses Highway N (11.92 mile / 37.32.023N, 90.51.688W).

The trail heads up the last of the big climbs for about a half-mile before reaching the top (12.40 mile / 37.32.081N, 90.51.207W). The trail travels across this ridge .40 miles, and then makes a steep, rocky descent. Pass a sign showing the direction of the Shut-Ins Trail and the Ozark Trail (13.76 mile / 37.31.826N, 90.50.604W). Both will take you to the parking area at the Johnson's Shut-Ins State Park. Following the Ozark Trail, it reaches the bottom and the trail is down next to the East Fork of the Black River (13.91 mile / 37.31.902N, 90.50.561W). Along the river the trail is mostly flat with a few small rises. It bends back into the woods on to a narrower path (13.98 mile / 37.31.981N, 90.50.503W).

The river is along the right side of the trail and you can get a view of the river bluffs through the trees. Soon the trail begins going up a steep climb. This climb is close to straight up the rock bluff and near the top be sure to catch your breath and take in the last great view, a WOW! spot (14.33 mile / 37.32.220N, 90.50.291W). Continue up the switchbacks to climb out of the river valley. The trail comes to a split (14.40 mile / 37.32.239N, 90.50.310W). The Ozark Trail continues to the left on the "red trail". In a short distance you pass a sign that says the parking lot is .5 miles and then the trail becomes a paved trail. The trail exits the woods and the parking lot is to the left along with the park store (14.70 mile). The park store is open Memorial Day weekend through Labor Day weekend. During the months of April and May it is open for limited hours and it is closed November through March. The campground is just a short walk that can be reached on a trail through the parking lot or by taking the road.

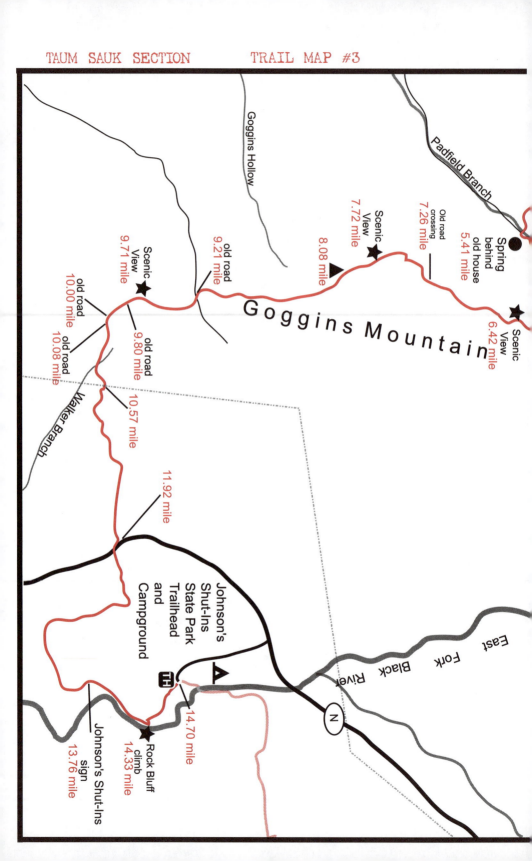

Goggins Hollow

Padfield Branch

Spring
behind
old house
5.41 mile

Old road
crossing
7.26 mile

Scenic
View
7.72 mile

8.08 mile

Scenic
View
6.42 mile

Scenic
View
9.71 mile

old road
9.21 mile

old road
9.80 mile

old road
10.00 mile

old road
10.08 mile

10.57 mile

Walker Branch

G o g g i n s   M o u n t a i n

11.92 mile

Johnson's
Shut-Ins
State Park
Trailhead
and
Campground

East   Fork   Black   River

N

14.70 mile

Rock Bluff
climb
14.33 mile

Johnson's Shut-Ins
sign
13.76 mile

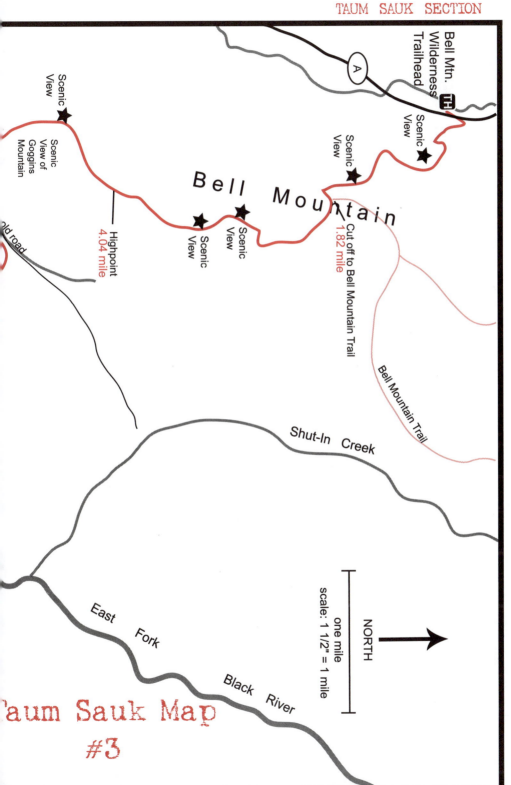

Bell Mtn.
Wilderness
Trailhead

A

Scenic
View

Scenic
View

Scenic
View

Scenic
View

Scenic
View

Scenic
View of
Goggins
Mountain

Scenic
View

B e l l    M o u n t a i n

Highpoint
4.04 mile

Cut off to Bell Mountain Trail
1.82 mile

old road

Bell Mountain Trail

Shut-In   Creek

East
Fork

Black    River

NORTH

one mile
scale: 1 1/2" = 1 mile

Taum Sauk Map
#3

Prickly Pear Cactus blooming in a glade on the Taum Sauk Section of the Ozark Trail.

# Trail Notes

The view of Marble Creek from the
Highway E bridge.

# MARBLE CREEK
## Section

DISTANCE: 8.25 MILES
TRAIL USERS foot, bike, horse

## ABOUT THIS SECTION

Before leaving the Marble Creek Campground be sure to check out Marble Creek. You'll find colorful dolomite boulders, mini shut-ins and the remains of an old gristmill dam.

This section of the Ozark Trail starts at the Trailhead parking area at the National Forest Service Marble Creek Recreation Area and Campground, located on the north side of highway E, just west of Marble Creek. The OT is accessed on the south side of E, and travels southwest towards Crane Lake. The trail travels through a hardwoods forest and crosses two creeks. At normal water levels the crossings are easy to manage and keep the feet dry. In wet conditions these creeks and ravines can become torrent water flows.

After 6.5 miles, the trail splits. The trail to the right leads to the north side of Crane Lake, features some great overlooks, and eventually leads to the Crane Lake picnic area and parking lot. The other option at the split leads southward and crosses Crane Pond Creek. It skirts towards the spillway and dam of Crane Lake, then completes the southern route around the lake and ends at the Crane Lake parking lot.

Crane Lake covers 100-acres and spills over the dam into the boulder filled scenic Crane Pond Creek. The loop trail that

<u>MAPS</u>
USGS Quadrangle maps:
Des Arc NE, Glover

<u>CAMPING FACILITIES</u>
Primitive camping is allowed along this section on public land except at the Crane Lake Picnic area. Camp at least 100 feet from the trail but no more than 300 feet.

Marble Creek Recreation Area and Campground- 25 tent or trailer sites with a table, lantern post and fire ring. No drinking water. Vault toilets. (in season)

<u>NEAREST TOWNS & SERVICES</u>
Arcadia, Ironton.

encircles the lake and part of Crane Pond Creek makes for a wonderful day hike. There is a day use picnic area with vault toilets.

## HOW TO GET THERE: Trailhead Parking areas

**Marble Creek Trailhead-** Located southeast of Arcadia. From Arcadia go south on State Highway 21 one mile and turn left on State Highway E. Continue on E for 12.5 miles and the trailhead is located on the left, just before the bridge over Marble Creek. The Marble Creek Section of the Ozark Trail begins across State Highway E from the parking lot.

**Crane Lake Trailhead-** From Arcadia take State Highway 21 nine miles south and turn left on to State Highway 49. Continue 2.6 miles on State Highway 49 and turn left on County Road 124. Stay on CR124 for 3.6 miles and turn right on County Road 131. Go 1.9 miles and turn right into the Crane Lake Recreation Area.

Crane Lake Trailhead from the Marble Creek Trailhead go west on State Highway E for 3 miles, turn left on County Road 124. Continue on CR 124 for 2.5 miles and turn left on County Road 131. Stay on CR 131 for 1.9 miles and turn right into the Crane Lake Recreation Area. The trail goes through the picnic area on the north side of the lake.

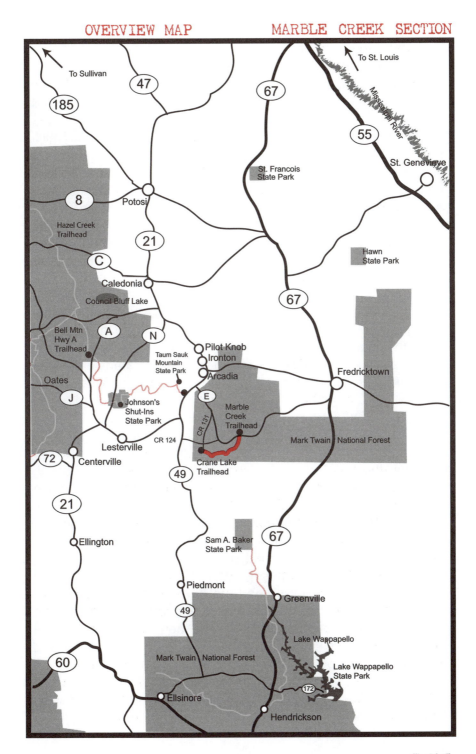

## Trail Description North to South

The trail starts at Marble Creek Recreation Area and Camp-ground Trailhead parking area (0 mile / 37.26.964N, 90.32.393W). Go across Highway E from the parking lot driveway and to the right where the OT goes into the woods. The trail begins in the forest and in a short distance begins to climb (.34 mile / 37.26.739N, 90.32.480W). The first part of this climb is gullied out. Continue up the hill. The trail bends to the left and is no longer gullied. Farther up the climb, there's a bend in the trail to the left and it gets a little steeper. The trail reaches the top of the climb (.67 mile / 37.26.564N, 90.32.483W). After a short downhill, the trail tips back up to where it is wider and gets some four-wheeler use (.74 mile / 37.26.477N, 90.32.496W). For the next .43 miles the trail contin-ues to have some small hills to a crossing of a dirt forest road (FR 2156) (1.17 mile, 37.26.174N, 90.32.643W). The trail goes straight across. There are no more signs of 4 wheeler use and the trail changes to single track. The trail is almost at the top of the ridgeline. Along the ridge line, the trail rolls up and down. The forest is mostly oak trees, hickorys and scattered pines. The trail starts a descent to a rocky creek bed that has a lot of ferns (1.78 mile / 37.25.765N, 90.32.920W). From here it's mostly uphill to the crossing of gravel road FR 2120 (2.21 mile / 37.25.680N, 90.33.306W).

After crossing the gravel road, the trail follows a two-track road (2.33 mile / 37.25.677N, 90.33.442W). Follow this for .04 mile and the trail turns off to the left (2.37 mile / 37.25.656N, 90.33.464W) and returns to being singletrack. From this point the trail heads down to a rocky creek bed (2.54 mile / 37.25.500N, 90.33.519W), that usually doesn't have water in it, but from the looks of it the water gets moving really fast here after a rain. The trail heads up to a forest road (no #) (2.91 mile / 37.25.420N, 90.33.826W). Cross the forest road. The trail continues through the forest to another forest road (no #) (3.19 mile / 37.25.401N, 90.34.087W). The trail turns to the left and follows the road. The trail stays on this road for .54 miles, and then turns off to the right on a small singletrack trail (3.73 mile / 37.25.008N, 90.34.211W). Keep your eyes open for this turn, as it can be easy to miss.

Just into the woods .10 miles there is a WOW! spot (3.74 mile / 37.24.99N, 90.34.223W). It is a nice glade area with mosses, lichens and rocks. The trail goes back into the trees (3.76 mile /

<u>Possible Day Trips</u>

This section is just over 8 miles long and makes for a great day hike (one-way).

Crane Lake Loop Trail 4.5 miles (round trip). This loop is designated as a National Recreation Trail.

<u>Contacts</u>
US Forest Service-
Postosi District
Highway 8 West
Potosi, MO 63664
573-468-5427

US Forest Service-
Fredericktown District
Route 2 Box 175
Fredericktown, MO
63645

37.25.042N, 90.34.250W). It is easy to miss this! Stay alert here and watch for the trail! At this point the trail begins a steep downhill to a small creek (4.02 mile / 37.24.968N, 90.34.436W). The trail continues on through a little grassy atv path then crosses a couple of dry rocky creek beds to a good uphill. At the top of this hill is the highest point on this section at 1,021feet (4.58 mile, 37.25.267N, 90.34.870W). In a short distance you'll come to a crossing of a forest road (no#) (4.61 mile / 37.25.268N, 90.34.893W). The trail makes its way down to CR 134 (5.10 mile / 37.25.041N, 90.35.292W). It's a gravel road and the trail goes straight across. The trail makes its way through the forest to the top of the next ridge and the crossing of another forest road (no #) (5.48 mile / 37.25.127N, 90.35.705W). After crossing the road the trail is wide and slightly downhill, then the downhill gets steeper. At the bottom of the hill the trail begins following a dry creek bed. The trail bends to the left, through a shallow winding creek bed. On the right is a creek that can have running water a lot of the year. After crossing the creek (6.10 mile / 37.24.811N, 90.36.342W) follow the trail out to the grassy field and turn left on the two-track path. You're now in Reader Hollow. In .40 miles the TRAIL SPLITS (6.50 mile / 37.24.811N, 90.36.342W) and there are two options around Crane Lake.

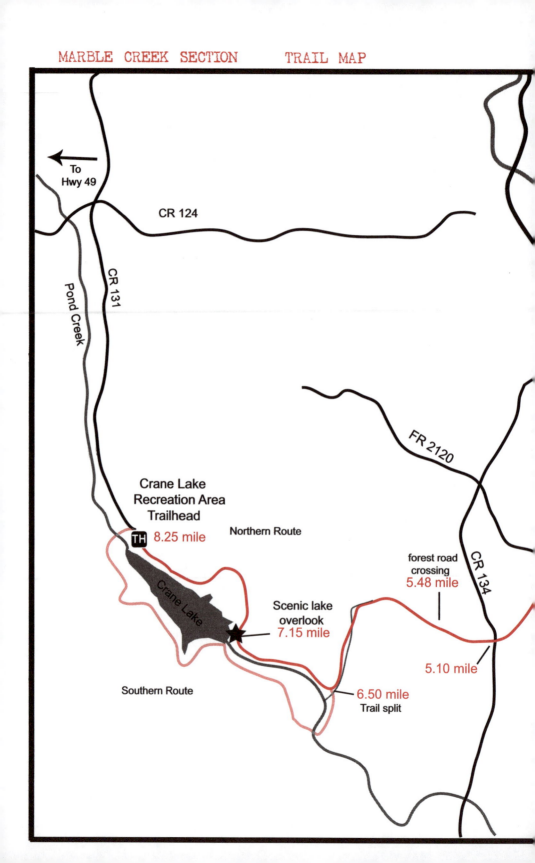

To
Hwy 49

CR 124

Pond Creek

CR 131

FR 2120

Crane Lake
Recreation Area
Trailhead

Northern Route

TH 8.25 mile

forest road
crossing
5.48 mile

CR 134

Crane Lake

Scenic lake
overlook
7.15 mile

5.10 mile

Southern Route

6.50 mile
Trail split

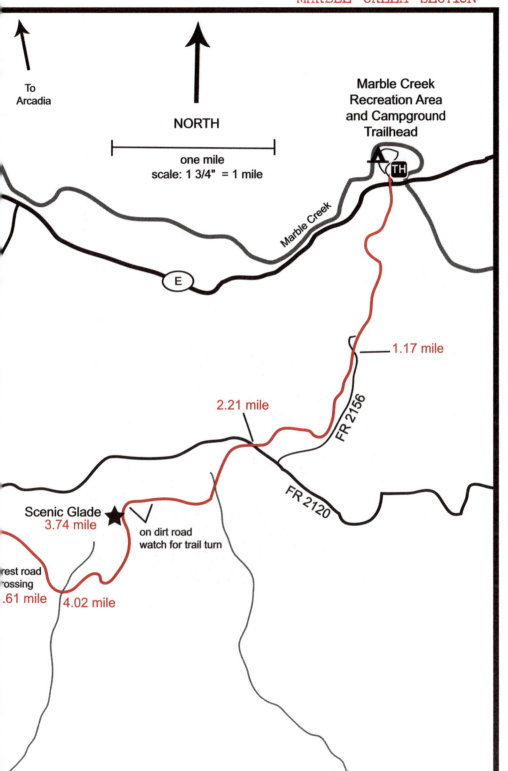

The view of Crane Lake from a rocky glade area
on the northern route.

## NORTHERN ROUTE

Turn right at the split to take the Northern route. A short distance from the split the trail leaves the edge of the field (6.65 mile / 37.24.885N, 90.36.469W) and heads into the woods. The next .50 miles is up and down through rocky ravines and along Crane Pond Creek. There are big boulders in the creek, and it's very pretty through here. In high water parts of this section of the trail will get flooded. The trail climbs up and out of the creek, and goes through some great rocky areas to the top of the hill and a WOW! spot (7.15 mile / 37.25.047N, 90.36.929W) with a view of Crane Lake. The trail makes its way up and along Crane Lake through the picnic area and to the parking lot (8.25 mile / 37.25.514N, 90.37.554W).

## SOUTHERN ROUTE (distances are from the split)

From the split, the Ozark Trail continues straight ahead to a creek crossing. Just past there, the trail is on old forest road (.03 mile / 37.24.756N, 90.36.347W). There is a barbwire fence and a field to left. There is a substantial creek on the right side of the trail. Lots of gnawed off saplings show the presence of beavers in this area. In a short distance the trail crosses Crane Pond Creek, where you'll probably get your feet wet (.27 mile / 37.24.587N, 90.36.426W). Immediately after crossing the creek, the trail comes to a "T". The Ozark Trail goes to the RIGHT. Just past the turn, the beaver dam is visible as you look upstream at the creek on the right.

The trail comes to a field and turns to the left. Then in about 20 yards, turn left into the woods away from the field. The trail veers to the right a bit, and you'll see a tree on the right with a silver diamond. Follow along the barbed wire fence (.44 mile / 37.24.656N, 90.36.557W) separating the woods from a field. Shortly, the Ozark Trail leaves the jeep trail and cuts to a smaller foot trail to the RIGHT. This is easy to miss, so watch closely (.48 mile / 37.24.667N, 90.36.589W). The ground is very soggy through here. The trail cuts to the left, to slightly more raised and drier ground (.62 mile / 37.24.793N, 90.36.623W). The trail continues .34 miles to where it starts going uphill to a rocky glade area with a view of Crane Lake (.92 mile / 37.24.908N, 90.36.885W). This pretty area continues for the next .10 mile with views of the bluffs on other side of the lake drainage. Also, there is a jeep trail running parallel just to the left of the Ozark Trail. The trail is very well marked up here. Soon the trail cuts to the right towards the dam.

After passing the dam and spillway (1.16 mile / 37.25.023N, 90.37.025W) the trail continues on to where it cuts to the right off of the jeep trail (1.29 mile / 37.25.008N, 90.37.167W). The Ozark Trail runs parallel to the jeep trail for a short while, and then the jeep trail turns away. The Ozark Trail skirts around a cove of the lake. The Ozark Trail re-joins the jeep trail (1.46 mile / 37.24.933N, 90.37.289W). Follow to the right. This will follow along most of the remaining length of Crane Lake. The trail bends to the right and crosses a drainage pipe (2.03 mile / 37.25.225N, 90.37.655W). In .5 miles, the trail crosses the concrete bridge over Crane Pond Creek that drains into the lake. Stay on the road after crossing the bridge (it looks like there's a side road that goes to the parking area, but it just goes into the lake). You will come to the entrance to Crane Lake Recreation Area (2.63 mile / 37.25.591N, 90.37.605W). Turn right and you are at the parking lot area. This is the southern terminus of the Marble Creek Section of the Ozark Trail.

# Trail Notes

_____
_____
_____
_____
_____
_____
_____
_____
_____
_____
_____
_____
_____
_____
_____
_____
_____
_____
_____
_____
_____
_____
_____
_____
_____
_____
_____

Horseback riding is extremely popular on the Wappapello Lake Section.(photo by Rita Glatzel)

# WAPPAPELLO LAKE
## Section

### DISTANCE 30.91 MILES
### TRAIL USERS foot, bike, horse

## ABOUT THIS SECTION

This section begins at Sam A. Baker State Park and travels south past Lake Wappapello State Park and ends at State Highway 172. This is probably the most popular section of the Ozark Trail for horseback riding. To accomodate horseback riders the trailhead parking areas are large enough to park and back up trailers. Much of the northern portion of this section is susceptible to flooding, especially when Lake Wappapellos level rises to 362 feet and higher. Calling the Wappapello Lake Project Office prior to traveling this section is highly recommended. (1-877-LAKE INFO)

## HOW TO GET THERE: Trailhead Parking area

**Sam A. Baker State Park Trailhead-** From Fredricktown go south on U.S. Highway 67 for 28 miles and turn right on State Highway 34. Continue for 4 miles and turn right on State Highway 143. Stay on State Highway 143 for 4 miles and the trailhead is on the right, or continue an additional .4 miles and turn right into Sam A. Baker State Park. The spur trail at the park is located off the park road near the entrance at State Highway 143 on the south side.

**Parking Area #53-** From the Highway 143 and Highway 34 intersection, go west on Highway 34 for 1 mile and turn left onto State Highway FF. Drive .3 mile and turn left (east) on County

MAPS
USGS Quadrangle maps:
Patterson, Greenville,
Greenville SW,
Hendrickson

CAMPING FACILITIES
Camping is permitted
along the trail in USFS
lands 100' from the trail.

Sam A. Baker State Park
Campground-
Camping, cabins, store,
showers, toilets, water
(in season). 573-856-
4411

Lake Wappapello State
Park Campground-
Camping, cabins,
showers, toilets, water
(in season). 573-297-
3232

NEAREST TOWNS &
SERVICES
Greenville, Hendrickson,
Poplar Bluff.

Road 380. Stay on CR 380 for 2.5 miles and turn left on an unmarked road, parking area # 53 is located .7 miles down this road.

**Parking Area #56-** This parking area is located on CR 380 3.4 miles southeast from Parking Area #53.

**Parking Area #58-** Located south of Parking Area #56 this area can be reached from Patterson by driving south on State Highway FF for 9 miles. Parking Area #58 is located just after the bridge over the Little Lake Creek and is on the left side.

**Highway 67 Trailhead/ Parking Area # 60-** From Greenville drive south on U.S. Highway 67 for 3.6 miles and the trailhead is located on the left. This trailhead is located near the grave of the unknown soldier.

**Highway F Parking Area-** From the Highway 67 Trailhead drive south on U.S. Highway 67 for 2.8 miles and turn left onto State Highway F. The trailhead is located 1 mile down State Highway F.

**Highway 172 Trailhead-** From Greenville travel south 14 miles on U.S. Highway 67 and turn left onto State Highway 172. The large parking area trailhead is located 1 mile down State Highway 172 on the left.

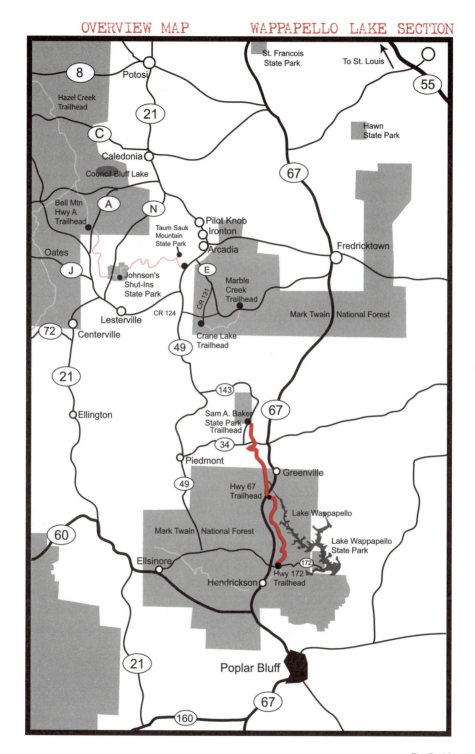

## Trail Description North to South

Begin at the spur trail in Sam A. Baker State Park near the campground. The trail starts on the south side of the park entrance road (0.0 mile / 37.14.189N, 90.30.788W). The trail can also be accessed south of here at the trailhead located on Highway 34. The Ozark Trail heads south between Highway 34 and the St. Francis River / Lake Wappapello. The trail comes to a small field. Go directly across the field and back into the woods. In a short distance a park nature trail meets up with OT from the left. Stay on the OT and it comes to a bamboo (cane) area. The trail comes out of woods and onto a small dirt road, (1.05 mile / 37.13.315N, 90.30.869W) turn left on the dirt road. In just a short distance the trail turns right back into the woods. Traveling in the "bottoms" the trail is pretty flat and can get very muddy as the trail heads west along Logan Creek. At 1.45 miles (37.13.140N, 90.31.128W) cross a wooden foot bridge over a small creek. Then cross a little dirt road. The trail goes almost directly across. You will come to the crossing of Logan Creek (1.53 miles / 37.13.081N, 90.31.189W). You can cross this in dry weather with barely getting your toes wet, but after rain it will be a wet crossing.

After crossing Logan Creek the dirt road continues straight, and the Ozark Trail cuts up into the woods to the left. Follow back along the south side of Logan Creek heading eastward. The trail leaves the woods and follows along the tree line at the edge of a field. The trail comes to a USGS metal marker and bearing tree (2.13 mile / 37.12.844N, 90.30.991W). In the next .2 miles there is an area that can get some very muddy spots. Come to a creek crossing that can have water, and a horse tie up. Pass several trees with yellow paint and eventually come to a bearing tree (3.23 mile / 37.12.184N, 90.30.617W). At the bearing tree you can see three more trees marked as bearing trees, and another metal land marker/monument. The trail continues in the forest for a short distance, and then enters a field. The trail is a bit of a trench in here. The trail returns to the woods, goes past a small pond, through an area with some cedars and comes to a spring (3.70 mile / 37.11.877N, 90.30.427W). The small spring flows out from under a big tree on the left side of the trail.

WAPPAPELLO LAKE SECTION

Now back along the river, the trail goes up and over a 'knob'. This area is very rocky, and the rocks are all oriented vertically, like they're sticking up out of the ground. It's a pretty spot. Just beyond the rise is an old, small 'out' building to the right of the trail. Then it's just a short distance to the crossing of Highway 34 (4.10 mile / 37.11.620N, 90.30.294W). Cross the road and the trail goes left down towards the river, paralleling the bridge for a short distance and then turns right into the trees. You'll cross over a grassy road (4.30 mile / 37.11.542N, 90.30.189W). The trail follows along the edge of the field, up and over the hill to where it enter the woods (4.53 mile / 37.11.429N, 90.30.349W). This part can be tough to follow because the tall grasses can easily obstruct the trail markers. Go down a small hill and through a deep ravine. This can be muddy and messy. The trail is now down in the bottoms and begins its way through some agriculture fields. The fields are mostly soybeans with a few corn fields. Keep your eyes open for OT markers through these fields. The markers get blocked by over grown vegetation and get knocked down. This makes navigating the fields difficult. Continuing on, the trail comes to a field opening (4.61 mile / 37.11.377N, 90.30.411W). Go to the right around the field for about 50 yards, then the trail turns into the trees. In the next field stay to the right. The trail cuts through some trees and into the next field (4.88 mile / 37.11.365N, 90.30.680W). Turn left and continue down 50 yards to

## Possible Day Trips

Highway 67 Trailhead to the Highway F Parking Area 3.9 miles (one-way).

Parking Area #58 to the Highway 67 Trailhead 2.5 miles (one-way).

## Contacts
Corps of Engineers
Wappapello Lake Office
10992 Highway T
Wappapello, MO 63966
1-877-LAKE INFO

Sam A. Baker State Park
RFD 1 Box 114
Patterson, MO 63956
(573) 856-4411

Lake Wappapello
State Park
HC 2, Box 102
Williamsville, MO 63967
(573) 297-3232

US Forest Service
Poplar Bluff Office
1420 Maud St
Poplar Bluff, MO 63901
(573) 785-1475

the next trail sign. The sign directs you to the right through an overgrown section that can get rutted, and has poison ivy. It is unlikely that this will be mowed. The trail comes out to the next field. At 5.25 miles the trail turns away from the soy bean field onto a two track grassy path that leads to a flowing creek.

Clark Creek (5.28 mile / 37.11.210N, 90.30.915W) is a mid-calf deep crossing. After crossing, follow the trail up to another bean field. Go left along the field and watch for markers along the edges of these fields. The tall grasses can easily block the markers from view. At 5.90 miles(37.11.092N, 90.30.897W) an OT sign marks a left turn, and takes you along another bean field. At Rings Creek (6.18 mile / 37.11.059N, 90.30.671W), cross the 6" or so deep clear running water. From the creek go up the small hill to another bean field. Go around the field to the left. At 6.30 miles (37.11.120N, 90.30.604W) an OT trail marker directs you to the right, past another soy bean field. Finally, an OT trail marker directs you to the right and away from the bean fields (6.70 mile / 37.11.130N, 90.30.147W). The trail comes to a marker (6.88 mile / 37.11.020N, 90.30.092W) with arrows pointing towards FF HWY. Follow the arrows and make the left turn. Ten yards from that sign the trail goes through a ravine and the trail is still 6-10 ft wide. Before long the trail turns into the woods and becomes single track, heading in a southern direction. Cross a power cut (7.13 mile / 37.10.996N, 90.29.943W). After the powercut the trail goes up to a small bluff with a view of the St. Francis River, then it heads to a very steep climb (7.55 mile / 37.10.621N, 90.29.819W).

Up on top of the ridge you will pass a wooden sign that says "Private Property stay on trail" (7.76 mile / 37.10.599N, 90.29.997W). The trail continues on this ridge and passes the sign marking the end of the private property and descends to a road crossing and Ozark Trail Parking Area # 53 (8.33 mile / 37.10.142N, 90.29.972W). It's a small parking area and turning a horse trailer around here would be difficult. The trail continues on a two track path along a bean field to a little wooded area, through two fields, and to an OT sign with an arrow pointing to the left (8.90 mile / 37.09.811N, 90.29.568W). Go left, through another field to where the trail turns to the right through another overgrown path (9.34 mile / 37.09.561N, 90.29.257W). The trail enters the bottom land forest and comes to a creek with a neat bluff (9.72 mile /

Dogwood trees bloom along the trail in April.

37.09.285N, 90.29.120W).  This spot is very confusing so watch closely for markers.  The trail cuts back across the creek to the right and into the trees (9.82 mile / 37.09.233N, 90.29.064W).  The trail goes straight up the hill.  Pass two bearing trees and a land survey marker, then descend to a usually muddy ravine in the bottoms.  After passing another land survey marker and two bearing trees the trail goes uphill.  From here the trail traverses the forest to a small creek 10 ft wide and 6" deep (11.00 mile / 37.08.527N, 90.28.561W).  Go up the hill and as the trail levels off, go towards the gate (11.10 mile / 37.08.438N, 90.28.606W).  At the gate and parking area the trail continues on the gravel road.  After .12 miles on the gravel road the trail comes to another small parking area (37.08.360N, 90.28.653W).  These parking areas are located off County Road 380.

The trail continues to the left on the grassy path.  The trail goes downhill and then up and over another hill to a bean field (12.22 miles 37.07.642N, 90.28.277W).  The trail stays to the right along the side of the field to where it turns right (12.43 mile / 37.07.412N, 90.28.366W).  Turn away from the field and go down an embankment.  Turn to the right on the two track path.  At Little Lake Creek (12.46 mile / 37.07.432N, 90.28.337W), cross the creek and go up the hill.  Watch for the sign about midway to the top of the hill and turn to the left.  The trail then turns and goes past a bean field and back into the woods.  In a short distance the trail goes across a creek.  After crossing, stay to the right on a grassy path.  Soon you can see the bridge on Highway FF.  The trail goes down into the bottoms and crosses Big Lake Creek (12.88 mile / 37.07.101N, 90.28.358W).  It's a short steep climb out of the creek.  Go right on what looks like an old road and up to the parking area at Highway FF and County Road 378 (13.02 mile / 37.07.011N, 90.28.332W).

From the parking area at FF and County Road 378 the trail goes into woods.  There is a short uphill, then the trail turns to left and follows a gated forest road.  In a little less than a half mile make a right turn off the forest road into woods (not a numbered forest road) (13.47 mile / 37.06.602N, 90.28.364W).  The trail continues .35 mile and has been following mostly southward.  At this point the trail makes a sharp turn to the left, then to the right.  The trail makes its way up to the crossing of Highway FF (14.51

Signs like this mark much of the trail through the
fields along the Wappapello Section.

To
Piedmont

49

A

Big Lake Creek

Parking #60
15.54 mile

Hwy F
Parking Area
19.40 mile

22.64 mile

Spring

Caldwell Creek

F

FR 3869A

CR 543

CR 546

67

25.32 mile

26.43 mile

CR 548 gate
28.39 mile

30.91 mile

Highway 172
Trailhead

172

17.44 mile
eastern loop
recommended

Lake
Wappapello

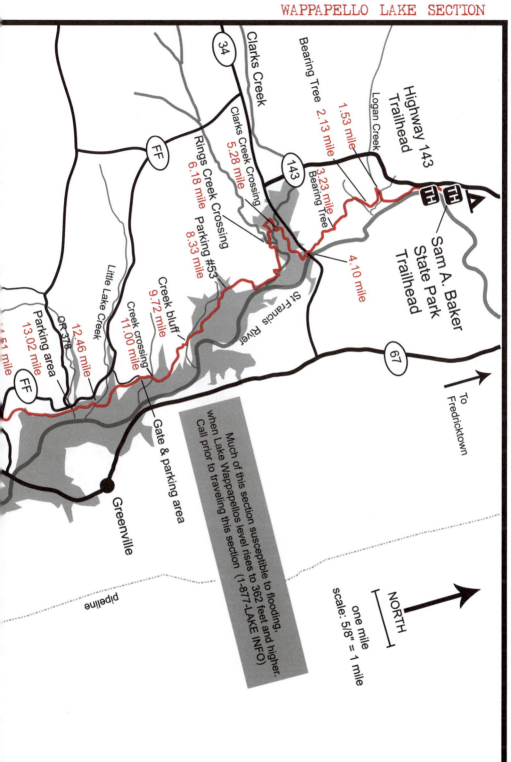

34

Clarks Creek

Bearing Tree
2.13 mile
1.53 mile

Logan Creek

Highway 143
Trailhead

Clarks Creek

FF

Clarks Creek Crossing
5.28 mile

143

3.23 mile
Bearing Tree

TH
TH

Rings Creek Crossing
6.18 mile

Parking #53
8.33 mile

4.10 mile

Sam A. Baker
State Park
Trailhead

Little Lake Creek

Creek bluff
9.72 mile

St Francis River

Parking area
13.02 mile

12.46 mile
OR 378

Creek crossing
11.00 mile

.51 mile

FF

Gate & parking area

67

To
Fredricktown

Greenville

Much of this section susceptible to flooding.
when Lake Wappapellos level rises to 362 feet and higher.
Call prior to traveling this section. (1-877-LAKE INFO)

pipeline

NORTH

one mile
scale: 5/8" = 1 mile

mile / 37.05.837N, 90.28.556W). Head downhill past a neat spot with tall, dense pines and to a forest road (15.16 mile / 37.05.429N, 90.28.420W). After crossing the forest road the trail continues fairly level to Highway 67. Cross the highway to the Ozark Trail Parking Area #60 (15.54 mile / 37.05.217N, 90.28.100W). This parking area is large enough for horse trailers to be turned around. The OT is not clearly marked at the parking lot. From 67 continue directly into the lot and straight up the hill. There's a marker a little bit up the hill. Before heading out on the trail you can make a side trip to the grave of the unknown soldier. Continuing on the Ozark Trail, at the top of hill the trail splits – eastern route goes left – western route continues straight ahead. **The eastern route is strongly recommended, as the western route was in need of substantial clearing.**

## EASTERN ROUTE

The eastern route is a little bit longer and is the most used trail here. The first 1.5 miles goes up and down through some pines. There is a small seep spring (16.21 mile / 37.05.150N, 90.27.592W). The trail leads to a rocky culvert. The rocks look like steps (16.59 mile / ) and there may be a small spring here. Just past this point the trail turns sharply to the right onto an old forest road. In the next mile the trail will pass a small spring-fed brook, climb a fairly long gradual hill and then head downhill to a creek. At the creek crossing (17.44 mile / 37.05.136N, 90.27.347W) look for a good place to cross up to the right, then go back to the left to re-gain the trail after crossing. From the creek, it is uphill to a powercut. Then the trail goes downhill to another creek crossing (17.63 mile / 37.04.434N, 90.26.878W). From the creek, the trail heads uphill and to the left. This climb follows Forest Road 3869A to where it splits (18.42 mile / 37.03.874N, 90.27.109W). The OT goes to the right. The trail heads downhill to a very small stream crossing, and just past there, to a dry creek bed crossing. After a long extensive climb, the OT levels off to Highway F (19.40 mile / 37.03.424N, 90.27.940W).

## WESTERN ROUTE

From the east/west split, after climbing another good hill the trail comes out on Forest Road 3771 (16.20 mile / 37.04.833N, 90.27.880W). The trail follows the forest road to the right. There are periodic silver diamond markers on trees on the left side of the road. The trail heads back into the woods on the left (16.41 mile / 37.04.747N, 90.28.048W). There is a trail marker on a tree on the left side of the road at the turn-in point, but this is not a very obviously marked turn. The trail goes downhill to a creek crossing, then through another creek bed. After this creek bed, the trail is very overgrown and is occasionally marked with silver diamond trail signs. The trail comes to another creek bed and follows the creek bed to the right for a short distance (17.73 mile / 37.03.760N, 90.28.019W). The trail will cross through another creek bed, then cross Forest Road 3771 (17.97 mile / 37.03.555N, 90.27.980W). After the forest road the trail follows a short distance along the north side of Highway F, then joins with the eastern loop and continues south across Highway F. The parking area is visible from here.

## TRAIL RE-JOINED

The Highway F parking area is very large, with enough room to turn trailers around (19.40 mile / 37.03.424N, 90.27.940W). The trail continues into the trees and heads downhill. The downhill gets very steep and very loose with pieces of chert rock on the trail. After .75 miles the trail gets down in the bottoms and is flat with some over grown areas. There are tall grasses and sticker bushes and a few stands of pine trees. Climb a small hill to where the trail levels off again. Cross a creek bed that had an old metal chair in the woods at the trail side then the trail starts to go up. At the top of the hill (20.36 mile / 37.02.660N, 90.27.848W) there is a view off to the left. The trail begins back up hill, and near the top crosses a power cut (19.54 mile / 37.02.382N, 90.27.883W). The trail travels up on top of a ridge. This is a nice oak forest. It comes to a two track dirt road, FR 3846A (19.74 mile / 37.02.214N, 90.27.804W). The trail goes straight across. Soon the trail turns a little to the right and goes down a hill. There is a short uphill then the trail continues back down and eventually passes a survey marker (20.72 mile / 37.01.941N, 90.26.967W). In .73 miles the trail climbs up to County Road 543 (21.45 mile / 37.01.344N, 90.26.861W). This is a gravel road without a parking area.

From the road crossing the trail goes downhill slightly past a small stand of pines and through some oak trees. The trail follows along a little gully with a lot of ferns growing. Here the trail is mostly level. Go through a dry gully and come to a creek lined with little ferns and moss. Climb a hill to where the trail crosses a very shallow gravel gully, and continue up and on a two-track trail. The trail comes to a very steep short down hill, then begins a steep uphill (23.04 mile / 37.01.023N, 90.26.796W). The grade of the climb lessens near the top and then the trail heads downhill. This downhill gets very steep. At the bottom of the hill, cross a small gravel ravine and continue along a grassy 5 ft. wide path. The trail comes to a field opening (23.65 mile / 37.00.767N, 90.26.351W). The trail marker points to the right and to the pipeline crossing. Go to the right and up the gravel road. Watch for the trail on the left-hand side of the gravel road before you go up the steep part of the hill (23.71 mile / 37.00.723N, 90.26.340W). The trail gets very overgrown here and is difficult to see the trail markers.

Just after getting back into the woods cross a small creek and go to the left on the grassy old two-track road path. The trail begins to gradually go uphill, then levels out, and begins a steep uphill. The top of the hill is up on a pretty ridge with occasional pine trees. The six-foot wide trail comes to dirt road FR 3044. Go straight across (24.20 mile / 37.00.445N, 90.26.077W). The trail

Land Survey Markers serve as reference points on maps and are placed in the outdoors by USGS survey teams. Coordinates and elevation are commonly engraved on the markers. It is unlawful to tamper with, destroy or alter any land survey marker.

begins back downhill shortly after crossing FR 3044. This downhill gets steeper. At the bottom of the hill, cross a little gully to a gravel ravine (24.64 mile / 37.00.128N, 90.25.883W), then the trail starts to go uphill. This climb gets very steep, but as you near the top it is a little more gradual. The trail comes to a road crossing and a clearing with powerlines (25.01 mile / 36.59.842N, 90.25.798W). At this point there is a small camp area. At the clearing go to the left on the small dirt road approximately 150 yards. The trail goes to the right. Watch closely for this spot where the trail turns back into the woods off the road. After cutting into the woods the trail goes downhill, then heads back uphill past a powercut and comes to County Road 546 (25.32 mile / 36.59.606N, 90.25.629W).

Cross CR 546 and the trail begins downhill. The trail comes down steeply and at the bottom of the hill the OT veers to the right. There is an old road/trail that goes to the left. Go a short distance and cross a small creek (25.95 mile / 36.59.106N, 90.25.545W). Just past here go by a lake on the left of the OT. The lake hooks around to the right, and the trail follows on the north side of the lake, then cuts southward on the west side of the lake. Go through an area of cedars and pines and you'll come to where the OT merges with an old forest road. The trail goes to the right on this road (26.26 mile / 36.58.956N, 90.25.786W). Just up the hill, the trail veers off of the old forest road and goes back into the woods to the left. The trail goes down hill. This is straight down to where it levels out at the pipeline (26.43 mile / 36.59.014N, 90.25.915W). Enter the pipeline cut, and the trail goes southward. There is a small shallow creek that you can step across, then the trail crosses to the opposite side of pipeline where it exits the pipeline cut and heads south. Follow along the eastern edge of the field. At the southeast corner of the field, turn westward and follow the southern edge of the field. The OT turns southward here and re-enters the woods (26.67 mile / 36.58.963N, 90.26.073W). There is a fiberglass marker at that turn, but it is not easy to see in the tall grasses. The trail goes about 50 feet into the woods then drops down into Otter Creek. This is a wet crossing and the creek looks as though it will have water all year. After the creek, the OT goes up a short, slick, muddy hill, then turns eastward back towards the pipeline. The trail is just on the western edge of the pipeline (26.83 mile / 36.58.877N, 90.25.978W), heading south. After a tenth of a mile the trail cuts east (left) across the pipeline cut. On the opposite side of the pipeline the trail continues south within the cut. After turning southward, there is a small muddy/swampy area. Just past the muddy area, the trail heads back eastward into the woods (27.09 mile / 36.58.674N, 90.25.937W). The trail goes straight uphill without switchbacks then straight downhill. Go up and down another hill, to more gentle rolling up and down hills and into the "bottoms". This area has vines, bushy growth and the OT levels out to where the trail opens up to very wide old road (27.75 mile / 36.58.458N, 90.25.500W). After a short distance, there are several very large boulders that prevent driving on this section. On the opposite side of these boulders is a gravel road, CR 548. The trail countinues southward on the gravel road. After .64 miles the trail leaves the gravel road, and goes to the left through a gate and back into the woods ( 28.39 mile / 36.57.971N, 90.25.791W).

The trail continues to a small creek crossing (28.52 mile / 36.57.900N, 90.25.869W). After the creek the trail starts to go uphill. The trail levels out, goes past some neat white rocks then leads to the crossing of Wet Fork Creek (28.61 mile / 36.57.854N, 90.25.936W). This is a big creek. The trail continues to the spur trail that leads five miles to Wappapello State Park (29.15 / 36.57.862N, 90.25.931W). Continue on the OT and you come to the crossing of a pipline cut. The trail goes straight across. The trail will pass a land survey marker and then cross Forest Road 3838 (29.90 mile / 36.57.057N, 90.26.650W). The trail goes along the flats and comes to the pipeline crossing that has a gravel road down the middle ( 30.22 mile / 36.56.879N, 90.26.521W). The trail goes straight across and just in the trees is a sign; Ozark Trail trailhead Highway 172 1/2 mile. From here it's a gradual uphill that steepens as you get closer to the trailhead. At the trailhead there is a very big parking area, with plenty of room to turn around a horse trailer (30.91 mile / 36.56.404N, 90.26.276W). The Highway 172 Trailhead is the southern terminus of the Wappapello Section of the Ozark Trail.

# Trail Notes

_____

_____

_____

_____

_____

_____

_____

_____

_____

_____

_____

_____

_____

_____

_____

_____

_____

_____

_____

_____

_____

_____

_____

_____

_____

_____

_____

_____

_____

_____

_____

Peggy Welch hiking through a Short Leaf Pine forest.

# VICTORY
## Section

DISTANCE 22.69 MILES
TRAIL USERS foot, bike, horse

## ABOUT THIS SECTION

The first part of the Victory section travels for 4.45 miles beginning at the southern terminus of the Wappapello Section. Then there is a gap of roughly 7.5 miles where the trail is not yet constructed. The Victory Section begins again across the Black River, across Highway 67, on the western side of County Road 404 (no trailhead there). The Wrangler Trailhead is 1.2 miles west of there, by trail or by road. Note that the first 3.4 miles heading west from Wrangler Trailhead were seriously damaged by a tornado in 2002, and this portion of the trail is not passable. Some efforts have been made to re-gain the trail, but it is still not possible to travel through this area. Directions for a detour by road are given. The trail description of this section is given from east to west.

## HOW TO GET THERE: Trailheads/Road crossings
## Trailhead/Road crossing Access Points

**Highway 72 Trailhead-** From Greenville travel south 14 miles on U.S. Highway 67 and turn left on to State Highway 172. The large parking area trailhead is located 1 mile down State Highway 172 on the left.

USGS Quadrangle maps:
Hendrickson,
Williamsville, Ellsinore.

CAMPING FACILITIES
Camping is permitted
along the trail in USFS
lands 100' from the trail.

Wrangler Trailhead
Campground-
Camping, fire pit, no
water, no toilets.

NEAREST TOWNS &
SERVICES
Hendrickson, Ellsinore,
Poplar Bluff.

**County Road 404 trail access-** (no parking here) From the crossing of the Black River at Hendrickson take Highway 67 south 1.87 miles and turn right on Mustang Lane. Then turn right (Pine Cone Estates sign) on County Road 402. County Road 402 is also labeled as Forest Road 3110. Go 2.9 miles on 402, then turn right onto CR 404. Go .3 miles. The trail picks up on the left side of the road.

**Wrangler Trailhead-**
From the crossing of the Black River at Hendrickson take Highway 67 south 1.87 miles and turn right on Mustang Lane. Then turn right (Pine Cone Estates sign) on County Road 402. County Road 402 is also labeled as Forest Road 3110. Stay on CR 402 for 3.4 miles and the Wrangler Trailhead is on the left, marked by a U.S. Forest Service Trailhead Sign.

**Upalika Pond Trailhead-**
From Hendrickson take State Highway 49 west 4.8 miles and turn left onto County Road 427. Stay on CR 427 for 2.3 miles and turn left on Forest Road 3112. Continue .4 miles and the trailhead is located on the left.

**The Brush Arbor Trailhead-**
This trailhead is located on County Road 427 just 1.4 miles south of the Upalika Pond Trailhead.

**Brushy Creek Trailhead-**
Located on State Highway V, 2.8 miles north of the city of Ellsinore

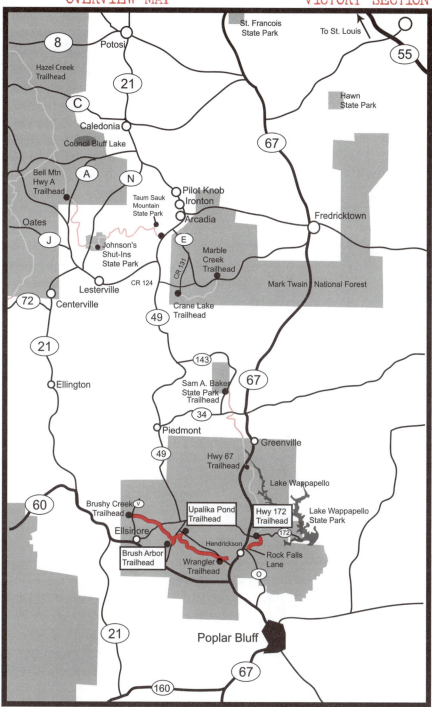

St. Francois
State Park

To St. Louis

8

Potosi

55

Hazel Creek
Trailhead

21

Hawn
State Park

C

Caledonia

67

Council Bluff Lake

A

N

Bell Mtn
Hwy A
Trailhead

Pilot Knob
Ironton

Fredricktown

Taum Sauk
Mountain
State Park

Oates

Arcadia

J

Johnson's
Shut-Ins
State Park

E

Marble
Creek
Trailhead

CR 131

Mark Twain National Forest

CR 124

Lesterville

72

Centerville

Crane Lake
Trailhead

49

21

143

Ellington

Sam A. Baker
State Park
Trailhead

67

34

Piedmont

Greenville

49

Hwy 67
Trailhead

Lake Wappapello

60

Brushy Creek
Trailhead

V

Upalika Pond
Trailhead

Lake Wappapello
State Park

Hwy 172
Trailhead

172

Ellsinore

Hendrickson

Brush Arbor
Trailhead

Wrangler
Trailhead

Rock Falls
Lane

O

21

Poplar Bluff

67

160

Possible Day Trips
Brush Arbor Trailhead to
Brushy Creek Trailhead
8.29 miles (one-way).

Brush Arbor Trailhead to
Upalika Pond Trailhead 2
miles (one-way).

Contacts
US Forest Service
Poplar Bluff Office
1420 Maud St
Poplar Bluff, MO 63901
(573) 785-1475

## Trail Description Highway 172 Trailhead to Rock Falls Lane

This section of the Victory Section of the Ozark Trail is connected to the southern end of the Lake Wappapello Section and travels 4.45 miles from the Highway 172 Trailhead to Rock Falls Lane. At Rock Falls Lane the trail ends abruptly at the side of this small gravel road. There is no parking area or trailhead on Rock Falls Lane.

Beginning at the Highway 172 trailhead the Victory Section begins on the south side of Highway 172. The trail enters the woods and travels .43 miles descending into the edge of Wolf Hollow. The trail then climbs steeply out of the hollow, and crosses a gravel road, FR 3704 (.60 mile / 36.56.042N, 90.26.101W). At the 1.03 mile point the OT reaches the spur trail that goes to Lake Wappapello State Park. It is 7 miles to the State Park. To stay on the Ozark Trail turn right. The next 1.2 miles of trail travels a relatively flat path through the mixed hardwood forest. Descend into the edge of Hockinberry Hollow and climb back out. At 3.07 miles (36.54.952N, 90.26.855W) the trail crosses through a grassy area (underground gas line). The trail crosses through this grassy area and curves down to the left to where the trail re-enters the woods. The trail travels mostly along a ridge line as it descends. Watch closely at the 3.62 mile point (36.54.669N, 90.27.317W). The trail makes a ninety degree right hand turn. This is an easy turn to miss! Another turn to watch for is at the 4.15 mile point (36.54.385N,

90.27.744W).  The trail turns off of the wider path, turning to the left onto a single track trail.  The trail descends .30 miles to where the trail ends at Rock Falls Lane (4.45 mile / 36.54.248N, 90.27.786W).

## Trail Description Northeast of the Wrangler Trailhead to Brushy Creek Trailhead

There is a gap of about 7.5 miles to where the trail starts again.  The next part of the trail begins at the west side of County Road 404.  There is no trailhead and no convenient place to park there.  From County Road 404 (36.53.564N, 90.31.948W), labeled as BC 404 on USGS topographic maps, the trail travels west along the Swift Creek bottomland.  It passes a power cut area and then climbs out of the creek valley.  The trail passes a bearing tree and follows along the edge of the hillside, the creek is visible below.  At the 1 mile point the trail crosses Forest Road 3738 (36.53.748N, 90.32.877W).  In a short distance a trail connects from the right.  Continue straight on the OT and to the crossing of Forest Road 3110, also called County Road 402 and labeled as BC 402 on USGS topographic maps.   Just across this gravel road is the Wrangler Trailhead (1.20 mile / 36.53.648N, 90.33.085W).

In April of 2002 a tornado ripped through the area between the Wrangler Trailhead and County Road 413 (BC 413).  This area has extensive damage, including downed trees, that makes 3.42 miles of the Ozark Trail impassible.  Work is continuing to be done to clear and re-establish the Ozark Trail in this area.  Before traveling this section of trail please check with the local Forest Service office for updated information.

The Wrangler Trailhead has a large parking area, and is big enough to accommodate trailers.  Camping is primitive, and water is not available. The trail leaves the parking area and travels west.  The next 3.42 miles is the tornado damaged area, the route is shown on the map for reference purposes only for when this section of trail is eventually cleared and re-established.

To bypass the tornado damaged area, turn left onto County Road 402 as you leave the Wrangler Trailhead parking area.  Go four miles.  Turn left on County Road 413.  Go one half mile.  This is where the OT crosses 413.  There is not an established trailhead here, but there are areas where a vehicle could park off the gravel

To
Leeper

pipeline

Black River

Middle Brushy Creek

49

Kelley Valley

16.21 mile

14.57 mile

TH
Brushy
Creek
Trailhead
18.24 mile

CR 447

CR 344

15.81 mile

V

A

Seed Tick Hollow

FR 3676

FR 3551

12.33 mile

FR 3812

11.82 mile

8.36 mile

CR 427

Upalika Pond
and Picnic Area

FR 3845

FR 3112

FR 3742

Dry

FR 3096

Ellsinore

6.52 mile

5.61 mile

Branch Creek

BC 413

60

TH
Brush
Arbor
Trailhead
9.95 mile

4.62 mile

Tornado Damage

To
Poplar Bluff

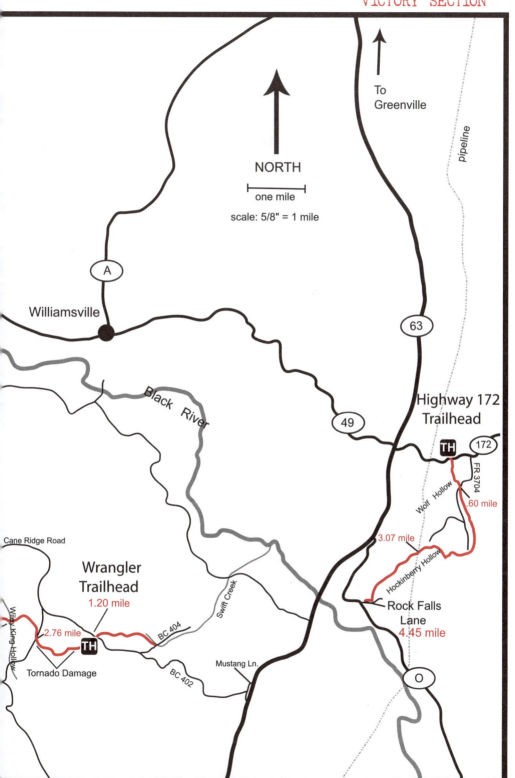

NORTH

one mile

scale: 5/8" = 1 mile

To Greenville

pipeline

A

Williamsville

Black River

63

49

Highway 172
Trailhead

TH

172

FR 3704

Wolf Hollow

.60 mile

3.07 mile

Cane Ridge Road

Wrangler
Trailhead

1.20 mile

Willey-King Hollow

2.76 mile

TH

Tornado Damage

BC 404

Swift Creek

BC 402

Mustang Ln.

Hockinberry Hollow

Rock Falls
Lane
4.45 mile

O

road. The trail can be followed from here westward to the end of the Victory Section at the Brushy Creek Trailhead.

The Ozark Trail travels west from County Road 413 (4.62 mile / 36.54.396N, 90.35.706W). At the 5.23 mile point (36.54.545N, 90.35.947W) watch for where the trail turns to the left and onto a wider path. Soon you come to a field that gets overgrown and has little signs of a trail when overgrown. Use caution here. Next the trail crosses Forest Road 3096, bends to the right and descends down to Dry Branch Creek (5.61 mile / 36.54.580N, 90.36.510W). For a while the trail actually looks like a creek bed and then continues uphill out of the creek valley. The trail passes a large pond that oddly has many bushes growing in it. The trail continues to a crossing of a small dirt road (5.83 mile / 36.54.700N, 90.36.670W). The single track trail goes straight across the small road and in a short distance the trail turns right onto a dirt road. Next the trail comes to the crossing of Forest Road 3742. Go straight across. The trail parallels FR 3742 and then crosses through a field. A camp area is located just after the field (6.52 mile / 36.55.199N, 90.36.862W). The trail crosses over the dam of a wildlife pond and parallels Forest Road 3112 to where it crosses an old dirt forest road (6.69 mile / 36.55.230N, 90.37.023W). The next .30 miles are a little bit tricky. Following the edge of a field and coming to a "T", turn to the left to stay on the OT. Forest Road 3112 goes to the right. The Ozark Trail travels west and downhill, crosses through a rocky creek bed then climbs uphill. The trail comes to an area that can get overgrown and turns back to the left. Cross an open area for maybe 20 yards (7.52 mile / 36.55.370N, 90.37.678W). In just .05 miles the trail crosses Forest Road 3815 (36.55.398N, 90.37.732W). The next .77 miles the trail crosses two rocky creek beds, then climbs up to the intersection with the spur trail to Upalika Pond and Picnic Area (8.36 mile / 36.55.857N, 90.38.086W). The spur trail is .41 miles to Upalika Pond and Picnic Area. This makes a good parking area for day trail travelers. Upalika Pond and Picnic Area is located on FR 3112.

At the intersection, turn left to continue on the Ozark Trail. The trail passes through an area with many small pine trees, goes through a deep three-foot ravine and then crosses an old forest road (8.96 mile / 36.55.794N, 90.38.518W). The trail continues to parallel County Road 427 and comes to a "T" intersection (9.3 mile / 36.55.548N, 90.38.671W). The Ozark Trail turns to the left here. The OT continues downhill the next .65 miles to the crossing of County Road 427, and the Brush Arbor Trailhead is just across this gravel road. On some older maps the Brush Arbor Trailhead is labeled as Walton Chapel (9.95 mile / 36.55.209N, 90.38.965W). The Brush Arbor Trailhead is a large parking area with plenty of room for horse trailers.

The trail leaves the Brush Arbor Trailhead and travels northwest, going through a field of tall grasses and pine trees. Some of the pine trees in this area are huge. The trail crosses a small creek that has small fish in it, so there is probably some water along here most of the year (10.50 mile / 36.55.595N, 90.39.158W). The trail begins to climb and comes to a left turn (11.08 mile / 36.55.960N, 90.39.547W). This area has many small pine trees. The trail descends for a while and then begins to climb and comes to the crossing of Forest Road 3812 (11.63 mile / 36.56.237N, 90.39.933W). After this road crossing the trail descends and crosses an underground pipeline clearing (11.82 mile / 36.56.371N, 90.40.020W). Just after the clearing the trail climbs up to the crossing of Forest Road 3551 (12.33 mile / 36.56.704N, 90.40.356W).

After the crossing of Forest Road 3551 the Ozark Trail continues westward and passes through an area with pine trees that has vines growing over them. The trail leaves the pines, bends to the left, and crosses Forest Road 3676 (12.71 mile / 36.56.821N, 90.40.722W). In .24 miles the trail bends in a northerly direction and turns left onto a wider path (12.97 mile / 36.56.882N, 90.40.937W). The trail travels .44 miles along the ridge line and then descends steeply into Seed Tick Hollow. For the next .65 miles the OT travels through Seed Tick Hollow and makes several creek crossings. This area can get overgrown and has many ferns and some Witch Hazel. The trail climbs out of the hollow and crosses State Highway A, which is a paved road (14.57 mile / 36.57.565N, 90.41.795W).

The trail goes straight across State Highway A. There is not a trailhead located here. The trail travels in a northwestern direction and in .14 miles the trail turns right onto a wider path (14.74 mile / 36.57.650N, 90.41.932W). The trail continues gradually downhill and crosses several small creek beds before crossing a good sized creek down in Kelly Valley. Just after this creek the trail crosses County Road 344 (15.81 mile / 36.57.975N, 90.42.754W). The OT climbs out of the valley and travels .40 miles to the crossing of County Road 347 (16.21 mile / 36.58.059N, 90.43.133W). The trail descends .56 miles crossing several small creeks that feed into Middle Brushy Creek. It comes to a larger creek that may have water most of the season (16.77 mile / 36.58.150N, 90.43.540W). At the creek there had been a small wooden bridge that was washed downstream. The trail travels through a lowland area, crosses several more creek beds, and then climbs up and over a ridge. The trail crosses a few more creek beds and begins uphill to where the trail veers to the right (17.42 mile / 36.58.424N, 90.44.009W). The trail climbs, travels in the woods parallel to an ATV path, and then comes to a split (17.77 mile / 36.58.400N, 90.44.352W). The OT goes to the right. At the 17.83 mile point (36.58.376N, 90.44.385W) the OT veers to the right and the less-used forest road goes to the left. On the downhill, the trail crosses County Road 352 (18.12 mile / 36.58.340N, 90.44.671W) and then crosses State Highway V. The Brushy Creek Trailhead is located just across State Highway V (18.24 mile / 36.58.364N, 90.44.752W). This is a large trailhead with plenty of room for horse trailers. The Brushy Creek Trailhead is the western terminus of the Victory Section of the Ozark Trail.

# Trail Notes

_____
_____
_____
_____
_____
_____
_____
_____
_____
_____
_____
_____
_____
_____
_____
_____
_____
_____
_____
_____
_____
_____
_____
_____
_____
_____
_____
_____

# About the Authors

Peggy is an East-Coast transplant to the Mid-West. She loves the wealth of outdoor exploration opportunities that Missouri has to offer. Peggy is a member of and volunteer for the Ozark Trail Association. She is also a chainsaw certified Forestry Service volunteer sawyer and helps to clear deadfall from the Ozark Trail. Her interests are photography, hiking, and fishing. She received her bachelor's degree from Mount Saint Mary's University in Emmitsburg, Maryland. She is currently the Vice President of Purchasing for Creve Coeur Camera in St. Louis. This is her first book.

Margo was born and raised in the St. Louis, Missouri area. She spent much of her time as a child and as a young adult on a bicycle. She participated in many BMX races, road races, and mountain bike races. Those experiences led her to write her first book, Cycling St. Louis. Margo has since turned her interests to the Ozark Trail. She is a member of and volunteer for the Ozark Trail Association, and serve on the Board of Directors. In 2004, Margo also completed the training to become a Missouri Conservation Department Volunteer Naturalist. Her interests include photography, studying Missouri plants and wildlife, hiking, and bike riding. This is her second book.

# *Websites*

The Ozark Trail Guidebook Online
www.ozarktrailguide.com

The Ozark Trail Association
www.ozarktrail.com

Danny McMurphys Hiking Site
www.fidnet.com/~mcmurphy1/ozarktrl.html

### Other Sites of Interest

www.ozarkbackpacking.com/ozark_trail.html
www.mostateparks.com/ozarktrail/
www.ozarkoutdoors.net
www.ozarkexplorers.com
www.hikearkansas.com/ohta.html
www.pioneerforest.com
www.missouri.sierraclub.org
www.greatgirlsbackpackers.myftp.org/index.html
www.usgs.gov
www.showmebch.com
www.backcountryhorse.com
www.fs.fed.us
www.ozarkgreenways.org
www.moniteausaddleclub.com/ozarktrail.htm
www.LNT.org
www.nps.gov/ozar
www.americantrailhorse.com
www.semo.net/suburb/fstenger/page2.html
www.hiayh.org
www.IMBA.com
www.USGS.gov

# Contacts

American Hiking Association
1472 Fenwick Lane
Silver Spring, MD 20910
301-565-6714

Bass' River Resort
P.O. Box BB
Steelville, MO 65565
1-800-392-3700
www.bassresort.com

Corps of Engineers
Wappapello Lake Office
10992 Highway T
Wappapello, MO 63966
1-877-LAKE INFO

GORC
Gateway Off-Road Cyclists
333 Atrium Ridge Court
St. Charles, MO 63304
www.gorctrails.com

Hosteling International
Gateway Council AYH
1021 S. Big Bend Blvd.
St. Louis, MO 63117
314-644-6192

International Mountain
Bicycle Association
PO Box 7578
Boulder, CO 80306
888-442-4622
www.imba.com

Lake Wappapello
State Park
HC 2, Box 102
Williamsville, MO 63967
573 297-3232

Leave No Trace
PO Box 997
Boulder, CO 80306
800-442-8222
www.LNT.org

Mark Twain National Forest
401 Fairgrounds Road
Rolla, MO 65401
573-364-4621
USGS Quad Maps

Mingo Saddle Club
P.O.Box 1027
Puxico, MO 63960

Missouri Department of Natural
Resources
Division of Geology and Land
Survey
P.O. Box 250
Rolla, MO 65401
573-368-2125
USGS Quad Maps

Missouri Department of
Conservation
P.O. Box 180
Jefferson City, MO 65102-0180
Missouri's Conservation Atlas

Missouri Ozarks Explorers
PO Box 747
Van Buren, MO 63915
573-323-8496
www.ozarkexplorers.com

Moniteau Saddle Club
2426 Pea Ridge Rd.
Centertown, MO 65023
www.moniteausaddleclub.com

# *Contacts*

National Park Service
P.O. Box 490
Van Buren, MO 63956
573-323-4235

Nature Conservancy
2800 S. Brentwood Blvd.
St. Louis, MO 63144
314-968-1105

Ozark Outdoors
Riverfront Resort
200 Ozark Outdoor Lane
Leasburg, MO 65535
1-800-888-0023
www.ozarkoutdoors.net

**Ozark Trail Association**
4835 S. Kirkwood #40
Kirkwood, MO 63122
www.ozarktrail.com

The Ozark Trail Guidebook
PO Box 358
Pacific, MO 63069
314-707-4422
www.ozarktrailguide.com

Pioneer Forest
P.O. Box 497
Salem, MO 65560
www.pioneerforest.com

Sam A. Baker State Park
RFD 1 Box 114
Patterson, MO 63956
(573) 856-4411

US Forest Service
Ava District
P.O. Box 188
Ava, MO 65608
417-683-4428

US Forest Service
Eleven Point Office
Highway 19
Winona, MO 65588
573-325-4233

US Forest Service
Fredericktown District
Route 2 Box 175
Fredericktown, MO 63645

US Forest Service
Poplar Bluff Office
1420 Maud St
Poplar Bluff, MO 63901
(573) 785-1475

US Forest Service
Potosi District
Highway 8 West
Potosi, MO 63664
573-468-5427

US Forest Service
Salem Office
1301 South Main
Salem, MO 65560
573-729-6656

Sierra Club
Eastern Missouri Group
7164 Manchester Road
St. Louis, MO 63143
314-644-0890

Show Me Backcountry Horsmen
www.backcountryhorse.com

# Gear List

map of area USGS Quad
compass or GPS
water and food
water filter
backpack
sturdy hiking shoes
first aid kit
tent
matches
raincoat and pants
sleeping bag
bug spray
trowl
cook stove
sleeping pad
hiking poles
cooking pots and tools
flashlight
camera
extra batteries for GPS and camera

Mountain biking
tool kit
tube patch kit
chain tool

Always let someone know where you are
going and leave an itinerary with them.

# Trail Notes

# MAP LEGEND

—————— Ozark Trail

Equestrians Allowed

Foot Traffic Allowed

Mountain Bicycles Allowed

TH Trailhead and Parking Area

★ Scenic Location

Campground

Trail Camping Location

Paved Road

Gravel or dirt road

River

Creek

Body of water

6.50 mile Trail Mileage

City / Town

Powercut / Pipeline